ChatGPT

Artificial Intelligence

While AI brings numerous benefits and advancements, there are certain topics that evoke concerns and raise ethical, societal, and existential questions. Here are some of the scariest topics associated with AI:

Superintelligence: The concept of artificial general intelligence (AGI) surpassing human intelligence raises concerns about its potential to outperform humans in virtually all cognitive tasks. The possibility of an AGI system becoming superintelligent and its implications on humanity's control and future is a topic of significant debate and apprehension.

Unemployment and Economic Disruption: The automation potential of AI systems can lead to job displacement and economic disruption. As AI technology advances, there are concerns about the impact on various industries, the displacement of human workers, and the need for societal adaptation and reskilling.

Ethical Dilemmas: AI systems may face ethical dilemmas in decision-making situations, especially in high-stakes contexts. The question of how AI systems should make ethically challenging decisions and the potential consequences of biased or unethical behavior is a critical concern.

Deepfakes and Misinformation: AI-powered deepfake technology can create realistic yet manipulated media content, including videos, images, and audio. The potential for malicious use of deepfakes to spread misinformation, deceive individuals, or incite conflicts poses a significant threat to trust, privacy, and societal stability.

Bias and Discrimination: AI systems can inherit biases from the data they are trained on, leading to biased outcomes in decision-making processes. This can perpetuate existing societal biases and discrimination, further exacerbating societal inequalities and unfair treatment.

Privacy and Surveillance: The widespread use of AI in surveillance systems raises concerns about privacy and the potential abuse of personal data. The ability of AI systems to analyze vast amounts of data and track individuals can infringe upon privacy rights and lead to mass surveillance.

Autonomous Weapons: The development of autonomous weapons systems powered by AI raises ethical concerns about their deployment in warfare. The lack of human oversight and the potential for unintended consequences or misuse pose significant risks to global security and stability.

Control and Manipulation: As AI systems become more powerful, the concern arises regarding their potential for being controlled or manipulated by malicious actors. The prospect of AI systems being used for cyberattacks, social engineering, or autonomous decision-making outside human control raises security and ethical concerns.

It is important to address these concerns and engage in ongoing discussions and research to develop responsible practices, regulations, and frameworks that ensure AI is developed and used in a manner that aligns with ethical and societal values.

The Author

Kevin Klein is an acclaimed AI engineer renowned for his groundbreaking work in the field of natural language processing and his extensive experience with ChatGPT. With a passion for advancing the capabilities of AI systems, Kevin has dedicated his career to exploring the intricacies of conversational AI and its transformative potential.

Throughout his journey as an AI engineer, Kevin has been at the forefront of experimenting with ChatGPT, pushing its boundaries, and harnessing its power to deliver exceptional results. His relentless pursuit of innovation has resulted in several notable achievements that have garnered widespread recognition.

One of Kevin's most significant successes lies in his pioneering experiments with fine-tuning ChatGPT for domain-specific applications. Recognizing the importance of tailoring AI systems to specific industries, Kevin ventured into customizing ChatGPT to excel in fields such as healthcare, finance, and customer service. His domain-specific versions of ChatGPT demonstrated remarkable accuracy, delivering personalized and reliable assistance to users in these specialized domains.

Kevin's expertise also extends to the ethical considerations surrounding AI technologies. He is known for his thoughtful approach in addressing bias and fairness in language models. Through meticulous curation of training data and employing bias mitigation techniques, Kevin has made substantial contributions to ensuring that AI systems, including ChatGPT, exhibit unbiased behavior and promote fairness in their interactions.

His work has been featured in numerous industry conferences and publications, where he has shared his insights and experiences in leveraging ChatGPT to enhance human-AI collaborations. Kevin's presentations have captivated audiences, inspiring other researchers and developers to explore the potential of ChatGPT and its impact on various industries.

Beyond his professional achievements, Kevin is recognized for his collaborative spirit and his commitment to fostering an inclusive AI community. He actively mentors aspiring AI engineers, sharing his knowledge and experiences to encourage the next generation of innovators. Kevin firmly believes in the power of collaboration and multidisciplinary approaches, advocating for diverse perspectives in AI development.

Kevin Klein continues to be an influential figure in the field of AI, with his innovative experiments with ChatGPT and his dedication to ethical AI development solidifying his reputation as a trailblazer in the industry. His contributions have shaped the future of AI and paved the way for a more conversational and intelligent interaction between humans and machines.

Overview

In this captivating exploration of conversational AI, Kevin Klein, an esteemed AI engineer, takes readers on a journey into the world of ChatGPT and its transformative potential. Drawing on his extensive experience and groundbreaking experiments with ChatGPT, Klein provides invaluable insights, practical guidance, and thought-provoking perspectives for readers interested in understanding and leveraging the power of AI in conversations.

Through engaging anecdotes and behind-the-scenes stories, Klein unveils the intricacies of training and fine-tuning ChatGPT, enabling it to excel in various domains. From healthcare to finance and customer service, Klein's domain-specific adaptations of ChatGPT have yielded remarkable results, delivering personalized and reliable assistance to users in specialized industries.

Beyond technical prowess, Klein delves into the ethical considerations that underpin AI development. With a keen focus on bias and fairness, he shares his meticulous approaches to curating training data and employing bias mitigation techniques. By addressing these challenges head-on, Klein ensures that ChatGPT and similar AI systems promote unbiased behavior, fairness, and inclusivity.

Throughout the book, Klein underscores the collaborative nature of AI development and the importance of multidisciplinary approaches. He emphasizes the need for diverse perspectives, fostering an inclusive AI community that encourages innovation, learning, and responsible AI practices.

"Conversing with Machines" is a comprehensive resource that covers a wide range of topics, including the history and evolution of AI, the training and architecture of ChatGPT, its language generation abilities, and the ethical considerations and challenges in human-AI collaboration. It explores the potential applications and impact of ChatGPT in various industries, offering insights into personalized content generation, code generation, and enhancing human capabilities.

As readers journey through the book, they gain a deeper understanding of the current state of AI technology, its limitations, and the exciting possibilities that lie ahead. Klein's lucid explanations and relatable storytelling make complex concepts accessible to both AI enthusiasts and professionals seeking to leverage AI technologies effectively.

"Conversing with Machines" is a must-read for anyone intrigued by the intersection of AI and human communication. Kevin Klein's expertise, passion, and pioneering experiments with ChatGPT make this book an essential resource for unlocking the full potential of conversational AI and its profound impact on our lives and industries.

CONVERSING WITH CHATGPT: EXPLORING THE POWER AND POTENTIAL OF LANGUAGE MODELS

Kevin Klein

CONTENTS

INTRODUCTION

In a world where technology continues to evolve at an astonishing pace, the rise of artificial intelligence (AI) has captured the imagination of individuals and industries alike. Among the many branches of AI, one area that has garnered significant attention is conversational AI – the ability of machines to engage in human-like conversations. At the forefront of this fascinating field stands ChatGPT, an AI language model developed by OpenAI.

In this groundbreaking book, we delve into the realm of ChatGPT and explore its capabilities, potential applications, and the impact it has on the way we interact with machines. Join us on a journey through the world of conversational AI as we unravel the intricacies of ChatGPT and unlock the power of human-AI collaboration.

Chapter by chapter, we embark on an exploration of the history and development of ChatGPT, tracing its evolution from its earliest iterations to its current state. We dive into the world of language models, understanding their training process, architecture, and the innovative techniques employed to enhance their performance.

As we delve deeper, we examine the underlying principles of natural language processing and understanding, shedding light on how ChatGPT comprehends human language and generates responses that align with context and intent. We unravel the mysteries of language generation, exploring its creative writing abilities, storytelling potential, and even its capability to generate code and technical content.

But the journey does not stop there. We navigate the complexities of context understanding, conversation flow, and personalized interactions, revealing how ChatGPT can adapt to dynamic dialogue, remember previous interactions, and tailor its responses to individual users.

Ethical considerations take center stage as we explore the responsible use of ChatGPT, addressing issues of bias, fairness, privacy, and security. We delve into the challenges of mitigating potential risks, promoting transparency, and building AI systems that align with our ethical values.

With a keen eye on the future, we reflect on the advancements, research, and OpenAI's roadmap for ChatGPT, envisioning the potential applications and impact of conversational AI in various industries. We explore its role in healthcare, finance, customer service, education, and beyond, highlighting the transformative possibilities that lie ahead.

Moreover, we empower readers to take the reins and embark on their own AI journey. From building chatbots to customizing ChatGPT's behavior, we provide practical guidance and best practices for integrating ChatGPT into personal and professional projects.

Join us as we navigate the intricacies of ChatGPT and the vast landscape of conversational AI. Discover how this remarkable technology is reshaping human-computer interaction, empowering us with new ways to communicate, learn, create, and collaborate. Together, let us unlock the potential of ChatGPT and shape the future of conversational AI.

WHAT IS AI?

AI stands for Artificial Intelligence. It refers to the field of computer science that focuses on the development of intelligent machines capable of performing tasks that typically require human intelligence. AI systems aim to mimic human cognitive functions such as learning, reasoning, problem-solving, perception, and language understanding.

AI can be categorized into two main types: Narrow AI and General AI. Narrow AI, also known as Weak AI, is designed to perform specific tasks or functions with a high level of proficiency. Examples of Narrow AI include voice assistants, image recognition systems, and recommendation algorithms.

On the other hand, General AI, also known as Strong AI or Artificial General Intelligence, refers to AI systems that possess human-like intelligence and have the ability to understand, learn, and apply knowledge across a wide range of tasks and domains. General AI remains a goal of ongoing research and development and has not been fully realized.

AI systems employ various techniques and approaches, including machine learning, deep learning, natural language processing, computer vision, and robotics, among others. These technologies enable AI systems to process large amounts of data, extract patterns, make predictions, and generate intelligent responses.

AI technology finds applications in diverse fields such as healthcare, finance, transportation, education, customer service, and more. It has the potential to revolutionize industries, automate repetitive tasks, improve decision-making, enhance efficiency, and create new opportunities for innovation.

However, ethical considerations, bias mitigation, transparency, and responsible use are crucial aspects that need to be addressed when developing and deploying AI systems. The responsible and ethical development and deployment of AI technology are essential to ensure its positive impact and minimize potential risks.

AI systems have a wide range of capabilities and can perform various tasks depending on their design and functionality. Here are some common applications and tasks that AI systems can accomplish:

1. Natural Language Processing: AI systems can understand and generate human language, enabling functionalities such as speech recognition, language translation, sentiment analysis, chatbots, and voice assistants.
2. Image and Video Recognition: AI algorithms can analyze and interpret visual data, enabling tasks such as image classification, object detection, facial recognition, and video analysis.
3. Data Analysis and Pattern Recognition: AI systems can process large datasets, identify patterns, and extract valuable insights. They are used for tasks like data mining, predictive analytics, anomaly detection, and recommendation systems.
4. Autonomous Systems: AI powers autonomous vehicles, drones, and robots that can perceive and navigate their environments, making decisions and taking actions based on sensor inputs and algorithms.
5. Virtual Assistants: AI-based virtual assistants like Siri, Google Assistant, and Alexa can perform tasks, answer questions, provide recommendations, and interact with users through natural language interfaces.

6. Healthcare Applications: AI is used in medical imaging for diagnosis, patient monitoring, drug discovery, personalized medicine, and assisting in surgical procedures.
7. Fraud Detection and Cybersecurity: AI systems can analyze patterns and anomalies in data to detect fraudulent activities, identify potential security threats, and strengthen cybersecurity measures.
8. Gaming and Simulation: AI is employed in gaming for developing intelligent game characters, opponent behavior, and realistic simulations.
9. Personalized Recommendations: AI algorithms analyze user preferences and behaviors to provide personalized recommendations for products, services, movies, music, and more.
10. Process Automation: AI automates repetitive tasks, such as data entry, document processing, customer support, and workflow management, leading to increased efficiency and reduced human effort.

These are just a few examples of what AI can do. As AI technology continues to evolve, its capabilities are expanding, enabling advancements across various industries and domains. The potential applications of AI are vast, and ongoing research and development are driving continuous innovation and new possibilities.

AI systems, particularly those powered by machine learning and deep learning techniques, are not traditionally "scripted" in the same way as traditional software programs. Instead of explicitly coding every possible action or response, AI systems are trained using large datasets and mathematical algorithms to learn patterns and make predictions.

In the training process, AI models are exposed to massive amounts of data, such as text, images, or audio, along with associated labels or desired outcomes. The models learn to recognize patterns within the data and make predictions based on the learned patterns. This learning process involves adjusting the internal parameters of the model to minimize errors and improve its performance.

While the training process provides the AI model with the ability to generate responses or take actions based on input data, it does not involve the traditional scripting approach of writing explicit lines of code. Instead, the model learns from examples and generalizes from the patterns it discovers.

However, it's important to note that AI systems can be guided and influenced through careful design choices and engineering techniques. Engineers and developers play a role in shaping the behavior and capabilities of AI systems by curating the training data, designing the architecture of the model, and fine-tuning its parameters. This process involves human intervention and expertise to ensure that the AI system exhibits desired behavior and aligns with ethical guidelines.

So, while AI systems are not scripted in the traditional sense, they are trained to learn patterns and make predictions based on data, and their behavior can be guided and influenced through careful design and engineering practices.

The hardware requirements for AI software can vary depending on the specific tasks and complexity of the AI algorithms being used. Generally, AI software can be resource-intensive and may require a combination of processing power, memory (RAM), and storage. Here are some key hardware components to consider:

CPU (Central Processing Unit): AI software can benefit from a powerful CPU, especially for tasks like training complex models or running computationally intensive algorithms. CPUs with multiple cores and high clock speeds are preferred.

GPU (Graphics Processing Unit): GPUs are well-suited for parallel processing tasks and are commonly used in AI applications, particularly for deep learning. GPUs accelerate training and inference tasks, and models optimized for GPU utilization can yield significant performance improvements.

RAM (Random Access Memory): Sufficient RAM is essential for running AI software effectively. Large datasets and complex models require ample memory to store and manipulate data efficiently. The more RAM available, the better the software can handle complex computations.

Storage: AI software may require significant storage space to store datasets, training models, and intermediate results. Consider using fast storage options such as solid-state drives (SSDs) to ensure quick access to data.

Networking: For AI applications that involve distributed computing or require data transfer across networks, a fast and reliable network connection is crucial to minimize latency and enable efficient communication between different components.

Specialized Hardware: Depending on the specific AI tasks, specialized hardware accelerators like Tensor Processing Units (TPUs) or Field Programmable Gate Arrays (FPGAs) can provide even greater performance gains. These hardware options are designed to optimize AI workloads and offer higher computational efficiency.

It's important to note that the hardware requirements can vary based on the scale and complexity of the AI tasks you're working on. More demanding AI applications, such as training large-scale deep neural networks or processing massive datasets, typically require more powerful hardware configurations.

Additionally, AI software often benefits from parallel processing capabilities, so having multiple CPUs or GPUs in a system or utilizing distributed computing across multiple machines can significantly enhance performance.

It's recommended to consult the specific hardware requirements provided by the AI software vendor or framework documentation for optimal performance and compatibility.

The concept of AI achieving self-awareness, often referred to as artificial general intelligence (AGI), is a topic of ongoing research and debate. AGI refers to AI systems that possess human-like intelligence, including self-awareness and consciousness. However, it is important to note that achieving true self-awareness in AI systems remains a significant scientific and technological challenge, and there is no consensus on when or if it will be achieved.

Currently, AI systems are predominantly focused on narrow tasks and specific domains, known as narrow AI or weak AI. They excel in specific areas but lack general intelligence or self-awareness. Building AGI involves developing AI systems that can understand, learn, and apply knowledge across a wide range of tasks and domains, akin to human intelligence.

The development of AGI involves understanding complex aspects of human cognition, consciousness, and self-awareness, which are still not fully understood. It requires significant advancements in fields such as cognitive science, neuroscience, and philosophy, in addition to advancements in AI algorithms and computing power.

While some researchers believe that AGI could be achieved in the future, the timeline for its development remains uncertain. Predictions about when AGI might emerge range from the near term to decades or even centuries into the future. It is a complex and multifaceted challenge that requires careful consideration of ethical, societal, and safety implications.

It's worth noting that there are also differing views on what constitutes true self-awareness and consciousness. Defining and measuring these concepts in AI systems presents additional challenges, as there is no widely accepted framework for assessing self-awareness in machines.

As research progresses and new breakthroughs occur, our understanding of AI and its potential for self-awareness may evolve. However, it is important to approach the topic with caution and continue to engage in thoughtful discussions about the ethical, societal, and philosophical implications of developing self-aware AI systems.

Several AI technologies have gained significant popularity and recognition due to their effectiveness and wide range of applications. Here are some of the most popular and well-known AI technologies:

1. Machine Learning (ML): Machine learning is a subset of AI that focuses on training algorithms to learn patterns and make predictions from data. It involves techniques such as supervised learning, unsupervised learning, and reinforcement learning. ML algorithms are used in various applications, including image recognition, natural language processing, recommendation systems, and fraud detection.
2. Deep Learning: Deep learning is a specialized form of ML that uses artificial neural networks with multiple layers to process complex data representations. Deep learning has been highly successful in tasks such as image and speech recognition, natural language understanding, and generative models.
3. Natural Language Processing (NLP): NLP enables computers to understand, interpret, and generate human language. It includes tasks such as speech recognition, sentiment analysis, machine translation, question answering, and chatbots. NLP technologies have become increasingly sophisticated, allowing for more accurate language processing and interaction.
4. Computer Vision: Computer vision involves AI systems that can perceive and understand visual information from images or videos. It includes tasks such as object detection, image classification, facial recognition, and image generation. Computer vision has found applications in

areas like autonomous vehicles, surveillance, medical imaging, and augmented reality.

5. Robotics and Automation: AI technologies are integrated into robots and automation systems to enable intelligent and autonomous behavior. These systems can perceive their environment, make decisions, and perform physical tasks. Robotics and automation find applications in manufacturing, healthcare, agriculture, and exploration, among others.

6. Recommendation Systems: Recommendation systems leverage AI algorithms to provide personalized recommendations based on user preferences, behavior, and historical data. They are widely used in e-commerce, streaming platforms, content recommendations, and personalized marketing.

7. Generative Adversarial Networks (GANs): GANs are deep learning models that consist of a generator and a discriminator network. They work together to generate realistic synthetic data, such as images, music, or text. GANs have been used for image synthesis, video generation, and data augmentation.

8. Reinforcement Learning: Reinforcement learning involves training AI agents through trial and error interactions with an environment. It is used to teach agents how to make sequential decisions to maximize a reward signal. Reinforcement learning has been successful in applications like game playing, robotics, and optimization problems.

These are just a few examples of popular AI technologies. The field of AI is constantly evolving, and new technologies and advancements continue to emerge, expanding the possibilities and impact of AI in various industries and domains.

ChatGPT, developed by OpenAI, is an AI technology that specifically focuses on natural language understanding and generation. It is a language model based on the transformer architecture and trained using large amounts of text data. ChatGPT is designed to engage in conversational interactions with users, providing responses and generating text that is contextually relevant and coherent.

While ChatGPT falls under the broader umbrella of natural language processing (NLP) and language generation technologies, its primary purpose is to facilitate human-like conversations. It incorporates techniques from machine learning and deep learning, including transformer models, to understand and generate human language in a conversational manner.

ChatGPT leverages its language modeling capabilities to interpret user inputs, generate appropriate responses, and provide information or assistance based on the given context. It can answer questions, provide explanations, offer suggestions, and engage in meaningful conversations on a wide range of topics.

The technology behind ChatGPT and similar language models enables applications such as chatbots, virtual assistants, customer support systems, content generation, and more. It enhances human-computer interactions by providing natural language understanding and generation capabilities, making the interaction feel more human-like and conversational.

It is important to note that while ChatGPT demonstrates impressive language capabilities, it has limitations. It may sometimes produce incorrect or nonsensical responses and can be sensitive to input phrasing or biases in the training data. OpenAI encourages user feedback to improve the system and address these limitations.

WHAT IS CHATGPT?

ChatGPT is an advanced language model developed by OpenAI. It is part of the GPT (Generative Pre-trained Transformer) series, which aims to generate human-like text based on the provided input. ChatGPT specifically focuses on generating conversational responses, making it well-suited for interactive and dynamic interactions.

As a language model, ChatGPT is trained on vast amounts of text data from the internet, enabling it to learn patterns, grammar, and contextual understanding of language. It leverages a transformer architecture, which is a deep learning model designed to process sequential data efficiently.

ChatGPT can understand and generate responses to a wide range of queries and prompts. It excels at generating coherent and contextually relevant text, providing meaningful and helpful responses in a conversational manner. Users can engage in dialogue with ChatGPT by providing prompts or questions, and it generates responses based on the patterns it has learned during its training.

It is important to note that while ChatGPT can generate impressive text, it has limitations. It may sometimes produce incorrect or nonsensical answers, be overly verbose, or struggle with understanding ambiguous queries. OpenAI continuously refines and updates ChatGPT to address these limitations and enhance its capabilities.

ChatGPT has numerous applications, including assisting users with information retrieval, creative writing, brainstorming ideas, providing customer support, and acting as a language-based virtual assistant. It has garnered attention for its potential to revolutionize human-computer interaction and improve various domains that require natural language understanding and generation.

HISTORY AND DEVELOPMENT OF CHATGPT

The history and development of ChatGPT can be traced back to OpenAI's ongoing research and advancements in natural language processing and artificial intelligence. Here is an overview of the key milestones and developments:

1. Early Language Models: OpenAI's exploration in language models began with the development of models like GPT-2, which gained significant attention for its impressive text generation capabilities. GPT-2 demonstrated the potential of large-scale language models but also raised concerns about potential misuse due to its ability to generate misleading or biased content.
2. Release of GPT-3: OpenAI's next major breakthrough came with the release of GPT-3, the third iteration in the GPT series. GPT-3, with its massive size of 175 billion parameters, set a new benchmark for language models. It showcased remarkable language generation abilities, including the ability to perform various language-based tasks, engage in conversations, and generate coherent and contextually relevant responses.
3. ChatGPT: Building upon the success of GPT-3, OpenAI focused on developing a variant of the model specifically designed for chat-based interactions. This led to the development of ChatGPT, a version of the GPT model fine-tuned for generating conversational responses. ChatGPT aimed to enable more interactive and dynamic interactions between users and the language model.
4. Research and Improvements: OpenAI actively engaged in ongoing research and development to improve the capabilities and address the limitations of ChatGPT. They leveraged user feedback and fine-tuning techniques to

refine the model's performance and ensure it provides more accurate, useful, and context-aware responses.

5. Public Availability and Feedback: OpenAI made ChatGPT accessible to the public through various iterations and releases. They sought feedback from users to improve the model's shortcomings and make it more reliable and aligned with user expectations. OpenAI launched ChatGPT in stages, starting with research previews and gradually expanding access to a wider user base.

6. Iterative Updates and Future Development: OpenAI continues to iterate and improve upon ChatGPT based on user feedback and ongoing research. They refine the model's behavior, address biases, and work on enhancing its conversational abilities while ensuring responsible deployment and minimizing potential risks associated with its usage.

The development of ChatGPT represents an ongoing effort by OpenAI to push the boundaries of natural language processing and create more sophisticated and useful conversational AI models. The aim is to develop AI systems that can understand and generate human-like responses, opening up new possibilities for human-AI interaction and applications in various domains.

APPLICATIONS AND IMPACT OF CHATGPT

ChatGPT, with its conversational abilities and language generation capabilities, has a wide range of applications across various domains. Here are some notable applications and potential impacts of ChatGPT:

1. Virtual Assistants and Customer Support: ChatGPT can act as a virtual assistant, providing personalized assistance and answering user queries in real-time. It can be integrated into customer support systems, reducing response times and providing automated support for common inquiries.
2. Content Generation and Creative Writing: ChatGPT can assist with content creation, offering ideas, suggestions, and even generating entire paragraphs or articles. It can be a valuable tool for writers, bloggers, and content creators to overcome writer's block or spark creativity.
3. Education and Learning: ChatGPT can serve as an interactive learning companion, providing explanations, answering questions, and engaging in educational dialogue. It can support personalized learning experiences, tutoring, and knowledge dissemination across a wide range of subjects.
4. Language Learning and Practice: ChatGPT can facilitate language learning by engaging in conversations and providing language practice opportunities. It can simulate dialogues and help learners improve their vocabulary, grammar, and conversational skills.
5. Personal Productivity and Organization: ChatGPT can assist individuals in managing tasks, scheduling, and organizing information. It can act as a digital assistant, helping users stay on top of their daily routines, reminders, and to-do lists.

6. Idea Generation and Brainstorming: ChatGPT can be a valuable tool for generating ideas and brainstorming sessions. It can prompt users with thought-provoking questions, provide alternative perspectives, and facilitate creative problem-solving.
7. Gaming and Interactive Entertainment: ChatGPT can enhance gaming experiences by providing interactive and dynamic non-player characters (NPCs) with natural language responses. It can create more immersive storytelling and dialogue-driven gameplay.
8. Research and Information Retrieval: ChatGPT can assist researchers, students, and professionals in information retrieval, providing relevant references, summaries, and insights on various topics. It can help users navigate vast amounts of information and access knowledge more efficiently.

While the impact of ChatGPT is promising, it also raises important considerations regarding privacy, security, bias, and responsible deployment. Safeguarding against misuse, ensuring transparency, and addressing ethical concerns are crucial in maximizing the positive impact of ChatGPT and similar AI systems.

As technology advances and research continues, the potential applications and impact of ChatGPT are expected to expand further, transforming human-computer interactions and revolutionizing various industries and domains.

UNDERSTANDING LANGUAGE MODELS:

Introduction to Language Models:

- Definition of language models
- Role of language models in natural language processing
- Importance of language understanding and generation

Training and Architecture of Language Models:

- Overview of training process for language models
- Pre-training and fine-tuning stages
- Architecture of language models (e.g., transformer-based models)

Natural Language Processing and Understanding:

- Basics of natural language processing (NLP)
- Language representation and embeddings
- Techniques for semantic understanding and syntactic parsing

Tokenization and Vocabulary:

- Tokenization process in language models
- Building and managing vocabulary
- Handling out-of-vocabulary words and rare tokens

Context and Sequential Processing:

- Role of context in language understanding
- Handling long-term dependencies in sequential data

- Recurrent and transformer-based architectures for sequential processing

Attention Mechanisms:

- Introduction to attention mechanisms in language models
- Self-attention and multi-head attention
- Importance of attention for capturing context and relationships

Evaluation Metrics for Language Models:

- Common evaluation metrics for language models
- Perplexity, BLEU score, and other relevant measures
- Challenges and limitations in evaluating language models

Transfer Learning and Fine-tuning:

- Concepts of transfer learning and fine-tuning in language models
- Benefits of pre-training on large-scale data
- Adapting language models to specific tasks and domains

Domain Adaptation and Specialized Language Models:

- Techniques for domain adaptation in language models
- Training models for specific industries or domains
- Specialized language models for technical, medical, or legal domains

Interpreting and Debugging Language Models:

- Techniques for interpreting and understanding language model outputs

- Attention visualization and saliency maps
- Analyzing model biases and addressing them

Continual Learning and Lifelong Language Models:

- Challenges and approaches to continual learning in language models
- Building lifelong language models with cumulative knowledge
- Balancing stability and adaptability in continual learning

As language models play a central role in many natural language processing tasks, understanding their training, architecture, and underlying principles is essential for harnessing their power and advancing the field.

Introduction to Language Models: Language models are computational models designed to understand and generate human language. They are a fundamental component of natural language processing (NLP) systems, enabling machines to comprehend and generate text in a way that mimics human language abilities. Language models play a crucial role in various applications, including machine translation, speech recognition, sentiment analysis, and chatbot development.

Training and Architecture of Language Models: Language models undergo a two-step process: pre-training and fine-tuning. During pre-training, models are exposed to vast amounts of text data to learn the statistical patterns and relationships within language. This process involves training on a diverse range of internet text to acquire a broad understanding of grammar, context, and knowledge. Fine-tuning follows, where models are trained on specific tasks with labeled data to adapt their knowledge and improve performance.

The architecture of language models has seen significant advancements, with transformer-based models gaining prominence. Transformers employ self-attention mechanisms, allowing the model to focus on relevant parts of the input sequence and capture long-range dependencies efficiently. This architecture revolutionized language modeling, enabling the generation of more contextually coherent and accurate text.

Natural Language Processing and Understanding: Natural language processing (NLP) is a subfield of artificial intelligence that focuses on the interaction between computers and human language. Language models play a crucial role in NLP tasks such as sentiment analysis, named entity recognition, and text classification. Understanding natural language involves techniques like semantic understanding, syntactic parsing, and discourse analysis, enabling machines to grasp meaning, context, and intent in text data.

Tokenization and Vocabulary: Tokenization is the process of breaking text into smaller units, or tokens, such as words or subwords, to facilitate language model processing. Vocabulary management is crucial, as language models operate on a fixed vocabulary. Handling out-of-vocabulary words and rare tokens requires specific techniques to ensure robust performance and accurate understanding of text.

Context and Sequential Processing: Language models excel at capturing context in sequential data. They leverage context to understand dependencies between words and generate coherent text. Recurrent neural networks (RNNs) were commonly used for sequential processing, but transformer-based models, with their attention mechanisms, have shown superior performance in modeling long-term dependencies and capturing context effectively.

Attention Mechanisms: Attention mechanisms are a critical component of transformer-based models. They enable the model to focus on different parts of the input sequence when generating text, mimicking human attention. Self-attention and multi-head attention mechanisms allow the model to weigh the importance of each word in the context, improving the quality of generated text and capturing relevant information effectively.

Evaluation Metrics for Language Models: Evaluating language models is essential to assess their performance and compare different models. Common evaluation metrics include perplexity, which measures how well the model predicts the next word in a sequence, and BLEU (Bilingual Evaluation Understudy) score, which evaluates the quality of machine translations. However, evaluating language models comprehensively remains a challenge, and researchers continue to explore new metrics and approaches.

Transfer Learning and Fine-tuning: Transfer learning is a technique where pre-trained models are leveraged for downstream tasks. Language models benefit from pre-training on vast amounts of data, which provides them with a broad understanding of language. Fine-tuning involves adapting the pre-trained model to a specific task or domain using task-specific labeled data, resulting in improved performance and reduced training time.

Domain Adaptation and Specialized Language Models: Language models can be adapted to specific domains through techniques like domain adaptation. Models can be trained on domain-specific data, allowing them to excel in industry-specific or specialized domains like medicine, law, or technical fields. These specialized language models improve the accuracy and relevance of generated text within their respective domains.

Interpreting and Debugging Language Models: Interpreting language model outputs is essential for understanding their behavior and ensuring reliable performance. Techniques like attention visualization and saliency maps help interpret how the model attends to different parts of the input sequence. Analyzing model biases and addressing them is an important aspect of responsible AI development and mitigating unintended consequences.

Continual Learning and Lifelong Language Models: Continual learning focuses on training models that can adapt and learn continuously from new data while retaining previously acquired knowledge. Lifelong language models aim to build systems that accumulate knowledge over time, allowing them to provide more accurate and context-aware responses. Balancing stability and adaptability in continual learning is an active area of research in the development of lifelong language models.

Understanding language models, their training, architecture, and underlying principles is crucial for researchers, developers, and practitioners working with natural language processing. It enables the harnessing of their capabilities, pushing the boundaries of language understanding and generation to create more sophisticated and useful applications.

INTRODUCTION TO LANGUAGE MODELS

Language models are computational models designed to understand and generate human language. They are a fundamental component of natural language processing (NLP) systems, enabling machines to comprehend and generate text in a way that mimics human language abilities.

Language models are trained on large amounts of text data, such as books, articles, and internet text, to learn the statistical patterns and relationships within language. This training allows them to acquire knowledge about grammar, syntax, and context, enabling them to generate coherent and contextually relevant text.

The main objective of language models is to predict the likelihood of a sequence of words or generate new text based on the given context. By capturing the statistical regularities and dependencies in language, these models can generate text that is grammatically correct and contextually appropriate.

Language models operate at the word or subword level, where text is broken down into meaningful units called tokens. This tokenization process allows the models to process and understand the sequential nature of language.

The architecture of language models has seen significant advancements, with transformer-based models, such as the GPT (Generative Pre-trained Transformer) series, gaining prominence. These models utilize self-attention mechanisms to capture dependencies between words and generate high-quality text output.

Language models have a wide range of applications. They are used in machine translation, where they can generate translations from one language to another. They are also utilized in speech recognition systems, sentiment analysis, text summarization, chatbots, and many other NLP tasks.

It's important to note that language models are not limited to generating text but can also be used for language understanding tasks. By leveraging pre-trained models and fine-tuning them on specific tasks, language models can be adapted to perform various NLP tasks, including text classification, named entity recognition, and question answering.

As research and development in language models continue to progress, their capabilities are advancing, allowing for more sophisticated language understanding and generation. Language models are a powerful tool in the field of NLP, shaping the way machines interact with and understand human language.

GPT (Generative Pre-trained Transformer) language models are a specific type of language model that has gained significant attention and popularity in the field of natural language processing (NLP). Developed by OpenAI, GPT models are based on transformer architecture and have shown remarkable performance in language generation tasks.

GPT models are trained in a two-step process: pre-training and fine-tuning. During pre-training, the models are exposed to massive amounts of text data, such as books, articles, and web pages, to learn the statistical patterns and relationships within language. This process helps the models acquire a broad understanding of grammar, context, and knowledge.

Fine-tuning is the subsequent step, where the pre-trained GPT models are adapted to specific tasks or domains using task-specific labeled data. This fine-tuning process allows the models to specialize and improve their performance on specific tasks, such as text completion, text classification, or text generation.

The key innovation of GPT models lies in their transformer-based architecture. Transformers utilize self-attention mechanisms, enabling the models to capture long-range dependencies and context more effectively. Self-attention allows the models to weigh the importance of different words in a sequence when generating text, leading to more coherent and contextually appropriate outputs.

GPT models have achieved impressive results in a variety of NLP tasks. They can generate human-like text, complete sentences or paragraphs, answer questions, and perform language translation. They have been particularly successful in creative writing, story generation, and chatbot applications, providing engaging and contextually relevant responses.

However, it is important to note that GPT models also have limitations. They may occasionally produce incorrect or nonsensical responses, exhibit biases present in the training data, and struggle with understanding ambiguous queries. Researchers are actively working to address these limitations and improve the performance and reliability of GPT models.

GPT language models have had a significant impact on NLP research and applications. They have opened up new possibilities for natural language understanding and generation, pushing the boundaries of human-computer interaction. With ongoing advancements and research, GPT models continue to evolve, paving the way for more sophisticated language models and applications in various domains.

TRAINING AND ARCHITECTURE OF CHATGPT

The training of ChatGPT follows a two-step process: pre-training and fine-tuning. Pre-training involves exposing the model to a large corpus of text data from the internet, allowing it to learn patterns, grammar, and contextual understanding. This process helps ChatGPT acquire general language knowledge and a broad understanding of various topics.

During pre-training, the model learns to predict the next word in a sentence based on the context provided by the preceding words. By training on massive amounts of data, ChatGPT learns to generate coherent and contextually relevant responses.

Fine-tuning is the subsequent step, where the pre-trained ChatGPT model is further refined on specific datasets and tasks. This process involves training the model on custom datasets that are carefully generated or curated to align with the desired behavior and domain-specific requirements. Fine-tuning allows ChatGPT to adapt its knowledge and improve its performance on specific conversational tasks.

Architecture: ChatGPT is based on the transformer architecture, which has revolutionized natural language processing tasks. Transformers utilize self-attention mechanisms to capture dependencies between words in a sequence and model long-range contextual relationships effectively.

The self-attention mechanism enables ChatGPT to assign different weights to different words in the input text, focusing on the most relevant words for generating responses. This attention mechanism helps the model capture dependencies and context, enabling it to generate coherent and contextually appropriate conversational responses.

The transformer architecture allows for parallel processing, making it highly efficient and scalable. It enables ChatGPT to handle sequences of varying lengths and generate responses in real-time.

ChatGPT's architecture includes multiple layers of self-attention and feed-forward neural networks. These layers enable the model to process and encode the input text, capturing the necessary context and information for generating meaningful responses.

It's important to note that the specific details of the architecture, such as the number of layers, hidden dimensions, and attention heads, can vary depending on the version and variant of ChatGPT.

OpenAI continues to refine and improve the training process and architecture of ChatGPT through ongoing research and development. Updates and iterations are made to enhance its conversational abilities, improve response quality, and address limitations to provide a more reliable and useful conversational AI system.

NATURAL LANGUAGE PROCESSING AND UNDERSTANDING

Natural Language Processing (NLP) is a subfield of artificial intelligence that focuses on the interaction between computers and human language. It involves the development of algorithms and models that enable machines to understand, interpret, and generate natural language text.

NLP encompasses a wide range of tasks, including:

1. Tokenization: Breaking text into smaller units, such as words or subwords, for further processing.
2. Part-of-speech tagging: Assigning grammatical tags to words in a sentence, such as noun, verb, adjective, etc.
3. Named Entity Recognition (NER): Identifying and classifying named entities in text, such as person names, locations, organizations, etc.
4. Syntactic Parsing: Analyzing the grammatical structure of sentences to understand the relationships between words.
5. Semantic Role Labeling: Identifying the roles of words and phrases in a sentence, such as the subject, object, or verb.
6. Sentiment Analysis: Determining the sentiment or emotional tone expressed in a piece of text, such as positive, negative, or neutral.
7. Machine Translation: Translating text from one language to another, preserving the meaning and context.
8. Question Answering: Understanding questions and generating relevant answers based on available information.
9. Text Summarization: Creating concise summaries of longer pieces of text, capturing the essential information.

10. Dialogue Systems: Developing conversational agents that can engage in natural language conversations with users.

Natural language understanding involves the ability of machines to comprehend and interpret human language. It requires techniques such as semantic understanding, syntactic parsing, and discourse analysis to derive meaning and intent from text.

Semantic understanding focuses on extracting the meaning and context from text, enabling machines to grasp the intended message. This includes tasks like word sense disambiguation, semantic role labeling, and understanding idiomatic expressions.

Syntactic parsing involves analyzing the grammatical structure of sentences, identifying the relationships between words, and understanding the hierarchical organization of language. This helps in capturing the syntactic dependencies and structural patterns within sentences.

Discourse analysis aims to understand how sentences and utterances are connected in a conversation or written text. It considers factors like coherence, cohesion, and the flow of information to interpret the overall meaning and intent of a piece of text.

Natural language processing and understanding have numerous applications, including information retrieval, sentiment analysis, chatbots, machine translation, and virtual assistants. Advances in NLP techniques and models, such as deep learning and transformer-based architectures, have significantly improved the accuracy and performance of language understanding systems, enabling more sophisticated and context-aware interactions between machines and humans.

BEHIND THE SCENES OF CHATGPT

Data Collection and Preprocessing: The development of ChatGPT involves collecting and preprocessing vast amounts of text data from the internet. This data serves as the training corpus for the language model. The collected text goes through various preprocessing steps, including tokenization, removing noise, and cleaning up irrelevant or duplicate content. The quality and diversity of the training data play a crucial role in shaping the model's language understanding and generation abilities.

Training Process and Techniques: The training of ChatGPT involves a combination of pre-training and fine-tuning. During pre-training, the model is exposed to the large-scale text corpus and learns the statistical patterns and relationships within language. The objective is to predict the next word in a sequence, allowing the model to capture grammar, context, and knowledge.

The training process utilizes deep learning techniques, specifically transformer-based architectures, which leverage self-attention mechanisms to model dependencies and context in language. This architecture enables efficient parallel processing and captures long-range dependencies effectively.

Challenges and Limitations: Developing and training ChatGPT comes with its own set of challenges and limitations. One significant challenge is handling biases present in the training data, which can lead to biased or skewed responses. Efforts are made to address these biases through data filtering, bias analysis, and fine-tuning techniques.

Another challenge is ensuring the model's response quality and coherence. While ChatGPT excels at generating human-like text, it can sometimes produce incorrect or nonsensical answers. Efforts are made to mitigate these issues through careful fine-tuning and model improvements.

Addressing Safety and Ethical Concerns: OpenAI prioritizes safety and ethical considerations in the development and deployment of ChatGPT. They aim to ensure that the system respects user values, avoids harmful or malicious behavior, and operates responsibly. User feedback is actively sought to identify risks, improve the system, and address potential safety concerns.

Iterative Improvement: ChatGPT is continually refined and updated based on user feedback and ongoing research. OpenAI releases updates and iterations to enhance the model's performance, improve response quality, and address limitations. This iterative process allows for the continuous improvement of ChatGPT's language understanding and generation capabilities.

The behind-the-scenes development of ChatGPT involves a combination of data collection, preprocessing, training techniques, and addressing challenges to create a language model that can generate contextually relevant and coherent responses. The focus on safety, user feedback, and ongoing improvements ensures that ChatGPT evolves and becomes more reliable and useful over time.

DATA COLLECTION AND PREPROCESSING

Data Collection and Preprocessing:

Data collection and preprocessing are crucial steps in the development of ChatGPT. These processes involve gathering a diverse and representative corpus of text data from the internet and transforming it into a suitable format for training the language model. Here's an overview of data collection and preprocessing for ChatGPT:

Data Collection:

1. Web Scraping: OpenAI employs web scraping techniques to collect a vast amount of text data from various sources on the internet. This includes websites, articles, forums, books, and other publicly available textual content. The goal is to gather a wide range of topics and writing styles to ensure the model's exposure to diverse language patterns and contexts.
2. Ethical Considerations: OpenAI is committed to ensuring ethical data collection practices. Steps are taken to respect copyright laws and terms of service for the collected data sources. Efforts are made to avoid biased or harmful content and prioritize the use of publicly accessible information.

Preprocessing:

1. Tokenization: The collected text is tokenized, which involves breaking it down into smaller units, such as words or subwords. Tokenization helps in processing and understanding the text on a granular level. Various

tokenization techniques are employed, such as splitting text based on spaces or using more advanced methods like Byte-Pair Encoding (BPE) or WordPiece tokenization.
2. Noise Removal and Cleaning: The data goes through a cleaning process to remove noise, such as HTML tags, special characters, URLs, and irrelevant information. This step aims to ensure that the training data is free from unnecessary artifacts and focuses on high-quality, usable text content.
3. Filtering and Sampling: To create a balanced and representative training set, certain filters may be applied to exclude specific types of content or to ensure an appropriate distribution of topics. Sampling techniques are used to manage the size of the training dataset, considering computational resources and optimizing training efficiency.
4. Language-specific Processing: Depending on the language(s) of the collected data, language-specific processing steps may be performed, such as lemmatization, stemming, or handling language-specific quirks and conventions. These steps help improve the model's understanding of the specific language characteristics.

Quality Control: Quality control measures are implemented to maintain the integrity and reliability of the training data. These measures include human reviewers who assess and label subsets of the data, ensuring consistency and identifying any potential issues or biases.

OpenAI emphasizes ongoing research and development to refine the data collection and preprocessing processes. They aim to improve the diversity and quality of the training data and mitigate potential biases or pitfalls associated with large-scale text corpus collection.

Data collection and preprocessing play a vital role in shaping the language model's understanding and generation capabilities. By curating a diverse and representative dataset and applying effective preprocessing techniques, ChatGPT can learn and generate text that aligns with human language patterns and contexts.

TRAINING PROCESS AND TECHNIQUES

The training of ChatGPT involves a two-step process: pre-training and fine-tuning. These steps utilize various techniques to train the language model and improve its language understanding and generation abilities. Here's an overview of the training process and techniques employed for ChatGPT:

Pre-training:

1. Objective: In the pre-training phase, the language model is trained to predict the next word in a given sequence of words. The objective is to enable the model to learn the statistical patterns and relationships within language. By predicting the next word, the model captures grammar, context, and semantic information.
2. Transformer Architecture: ChatGPT is based on the transformer architecture, which has revolutionized natural language processing. Transformers utilize self-attention mechanisms to capture dependencies between words and model long-range contextual relationships effectively. This architecture enables efficient parallel processing and captures intricate language patterns.
3. Large-scale Text Corpus: During pre-training, ChatGPT is exposed to a massive amount of text data collected from the internet. The data includes a wide variety of sources, such as books, articles, and websites, providing the model with a broad understanding of different topics and writing styles.

Fine-tuning:

1. Task-Specific Datasets: After pre-training, ChatGPT is fine-tuned on specific tasks or datasets to improve its performance on those particular domains. The fine-tuning process involves training the model on custom datasets that are carefully generated or curated to align with the desired behavior and requirements.
2. Labeled Data: The fine-tuning datasets are labeled with appropriate responses or annotations, depending on the task. For example, if the goal is to create a customer support chatbot, the dataset may consist of customer queries paired with corresponding expert responses.
3. Transfer Learning: Fine-tuning leverages transfer learning, where the pre-trained model's knowledge is transferred and adapted to the specific task or domain. This allows ChatGPT to benefit from the general language understanding acquired during pre-training and focus on task-specific learning.

Iterative Improvement: ChatGPT's training involves an iterative improvement process. OpenAI releases different versions and iterations of the model, taking user feedback into account to refine and enhance its capabilities. This feedback-driven approach helps identify areas for improvement, address limitations, and optimize the model's performance over time.

Ethical Considerations: OpenAI is committed to ensuring ethical considerations in the training process. Steps are taken to mitigate biases, avoid promoting harmful or biased content, and ensure responsible behavior of the language model. Continuous research and development efforts are made to enhance safety measures and address ethical concerns.

The training process and techniques employed for ChatGPT involve pre-training the model on a large-scale text corpus to learn language patterns and relationships. Subsequently, fine-tuning is performed on task-specific datasets to adapt the model to particular domains. These iterative training processes, combined with the transformer architecture, contribute to ChatGPT's language understanding and generation capabilities.

CHALLENGES AND LIMITATIONS OF CHATGPT

While ChatGPT demonstrates impressive language generation capabilities, it also faces certain challenges and limitations that are important to consider:

1. Contextual Understanding: ChatGPT may sometimes struggle to fully grasp the context and nuances of a conversation. It tends to generate responses based on local context rather than maintaining a consistent understanding of the conversation history. This limitation can lead to responses that appear plausible but may not accurately address the user's intent.
2. Incorrect or Nonsensical Responses: Due to the statistical nature of language modeling, ChatGPT can occasionally generate incorrect or nonsensical responses. The model lacks external knowledge verification and may generate answers that are factually inaccurate or out of context.
3. Sensitivity to Input Phrasing: ChatGPT is highly sensitive to the phrasing of user input. Slight rephrasing of a question or prompt can yield different responses, which may be inconsistent or lead to unexpected outputs. This sensitivity can impact user experience and require careful input formulation.
4. Biases in Language and Responses: ChatGPT's training data is collected from the internet, which can introduce biases present in online content. As a result, ChatGPT may inadvertently exhibit biases in its responses. OpenAI is actively working to mitigate these biases through research, data selection, and fine-tuning techniques.
5. Dependence on Training Data: The performance of ChatGPT heavily relies on the quality, diversity, and

representativeness of the training data. Biases, inaccuracies, or limitations within the training data can manifest in the model's behavior and responses.

6. Lack of Common Sense Reasoning: While ChatGPT can generate coherent responses, it may struggle with common sense reasoning or understanding specific world knowledge. The model does not possess true understanding or awareness beyond the statistical patterns learned from the training data.

Addressing these challenges and limitations is an active area of research and development for ChatGPT and similar language models. OpenAI actively seeks user feedback to identify areas for improvement, refine the model's behavior, and address its limitations. Iterative updates and ongoing research aim to enhance ChatGPT's performance, mitigate biases, improve context handling, and foster a more reliable and useful conversational AI system.

EXPLORING CHATGPT'S CAPABILITIES

ChatGPT possesses several notable capabilities that contribute to its effectiveness as a conversational AI system. Here are some key aspects of ChatGPT's capabilities:

1. Natural Language Understanding: ChatGPT can understand and interpret natural language inputs, allowing users to engage in conversational interactions. It can comprehend a wide range of topics and respond contextually to user queries and prompts.
2. Language Generation: ChatGPT excels at generating human-like text responses. It can generate coherent and contextually relevant answers, explanations, or creative content. This capability makes ChatGPT useful for tasks such as content generation, writing assistance, and interactive storytelling.
3. Contextual Responses: ChatGPT takes into account the conversation history and context to generate more contextually appropriate responses. It can maintain a basic memory of previous turns in the conversation, allowing for more coherent and meaningful interactions.
4. General Knowledge: ChatGPT has been trained on a vast corpus of text data, enabling it to possess a broad understanding of general knowledge across various domains. It can provide information, answer factual questions, and engage in discussions on diverse topics.
5. Sentiment and Tone: ChatGPT can discern sentiment and tone in user inputs, allowing it to generate responses that align with the emotional context. It can provide empathetic or neutral responses based on the tone of the conversation.

6. Multi-Turn Dialogue: ChatGPT is designed to handle multi-turn conversations, where it can maintain context and provide relevant responses based on the ongoing dialogue. This capability enables more interactive and dynamic interactions with users.

7. Assistance and Suggestions: ChatGPT can offer assistance, suggestions, and recommendations in various domains. It can provide guidance, propose ideas, or help users with tasks, making it a valuable tool for productivity and decision-making.

8. Language Adaptation: ChatGPT can adapt its responses to specific styles or tones based on user prompts. It can mimic certain personas or adjust the formality of its language, allowing for more tailored and personalized interactions.

It's important to note that ChatGPT has limitations and may occasionally produce incorrect or nonsensical responses. Users should exercise caution and critically evaluate the generated content. OpenAI actively encourages user feedback to improve the system's capabilities, address limitations, and ensure responsible use of ChatGPT.

By exploring ChatGPT's capabilities and understanding its strengths and limitations, users can leverage it effectively in various applications such as content generation, creative writing, language assistance, and interactive conversations.

CHATGPT'S LANGUAGE GENERATION ABILITIES

ChatGPT demonstrates impressive language generation abilities, which contribute to its effectiveness in generating human-like and contextually relevant responses. Here are some key aspects of ChatGPT's language generation capabilities:

1. Coherent and Contextually Relevant Responses: ChatGPT can generate responses that are coherent and contextually appropriate to the given conversation. It leverages its training on vast amounts of text data to understand language patterns, grammar, and context. This enables it to produce responses that align with the topic and flow of the ongoing conversation.

2. Grammar and Syntax: ChatGPT has a strong grasp of grammar and syntax, allowing it to generate text that adheres to linguistic rules. It can produce grammatically correct sentences and follow syntactic structures typical in natural language.

3. Contextual Understanding: ChatGPT considers the conversation history and context when generating responses. It takes into account the preceding user inputs to provide meaningful and relevant answers. This context-awareness contributes to more coherent and informed responses.

4. Creative Writing: ChatGPT can exhibit creative writing abilities by generating engaging and imaginative text. It can compose stories, provide vivid descriptions, and come up with novel ideas. This capability makes ChatGPT a useful tool for generating creative content and storytelling.

5. Language Variation and Style: ChatGPT can adapt its language style to match specific tones or personas. It can

mimic certain writing styles, adjust formality levels, or adopt different registers of speech. This flexibility allows for tailored responses that suit the desired language style or tone.

6. Conciseness and Summarization: ChatGPT can generate concise summaries or condensed versions of longer pieces of text. It can distill essential information and capture the main points, providing succinct and informative summaries.
7. Empathy and Emotional Tone: ChatGPT can understand emotional cues in user input and generate responses with an empathetic or neutral tone. It can acknowledge and respond to user emotions appropriately, enhancing the conversational experience.
8. Domain-Specific Language: By fine-tuning on domain-specific datasets, ChatGPT can exhibit language generation abilities tailored to specific domains. It can generate text that is specific to industries like medicine, law, or technology, making it applicable in specialized contexts.

While ChatGPT's language generation abilities are remarkable, it's essential to note that it has limitations. It may occasionally produce incorrect, biased, or nonsensical responses. Users should exercise critical judgment and verify the generated content when using ChatGPT for specific applications.

OpenAI continues to refine and enhance ChatGPT's language generation capabilities through ongoing research and development, addressing limitations, and incorporating user feedback to ensure more reliable and contextually accurate responses.

CONTEXT UNDERSTANDING AND CONVERSATION FLOW

Context understanding and maintaining a coherent conversation flow are crucial aspects of ChatGPT's capabilities. Here's how ChatGPT achieves context understanding and manages conversation flow:

1. Contextual Information: ChatGPT considers the conversation history to understand and generate responses in context. It takes into account the preceding user inputs, allowing it to maintain a basic understanding of the ongoing conversation. This context-awareness enables ChatGPT to generate responses that align with the topic and context of the discussion.
2. Conversation Memory: ChatGPT retains a limited memory of the conversation history to ensure continuity and coherence. It can refer back to previous user queries or responses, incorporating relevant information into its generated responses. This memory mechanism helps ChatGPT maintain a coherent conversation flow.
3. Response Relevance: ChatGPT aims to generate responses that are relevant and directly address the user's queries or prompts. It analyzes the input and identifies the main intent or topic to ensure that the generated response aligns with the user's expectation and maintains the flow of the conversation.
4. Generating Follow-up Questions: In multi-turn conversations, ChatGPT can generate follow-up questions to seek clarification or further engage the user. By asking relevant questions, it facilitates the flow of the conversation and encourages more interactive and meaningful interactions.

5. Context Shift Handling: ChatGPT is designed to handle context shifts in conversations. It can adapt its responses when the topic or context changes within the conversation. This adaptability allows ChatGPT to smoothly transition between different subjects and maintain the coherence of the conversation.
6. Handling User Corrections: If a user provides feedback or corrects a response, ChatGPT can adjust its subsequent replies accordingly. It takes user corrections into account to improve the accuracy and relevance of its generated responses, facilitating a more effective conversation flow.
7. Long-term Coherence: ChatGPT leverages its training on large-scale text data to understand long-term dependencies and maintain coherence throughout the conversation. It captures contextual relationships and patterns from the training data to generate responses that are contextually appropriate and maintain a coherent flow of information.

It's important to note that while ChatGPT makes efforts to understand and maintain conversation flow, it may occasionally lose track of the context, leading to responses that may not align perfectly with the user's intent or the ongoing conversation. Users should provide clear and concise prompts to enhance context understanding and help ChatGPT generate more accurate and relevant responses.

OpenAI continues to refine and improve ChatGPT's context understanding capabilities through ongoing research and development, aiming to provide more seamless and coherent conversations between users and the system.

CREATIVE WRITING AND STORYTELLING WITH CHATGPT

ChatGPT can be a valuable tool for creative writing and storytelling, offering assistance and generating imaginative content. Here's how ChatGPT can be utilized for creative writing and storytelling purposes:

1. Story Generation: ChatGPT can generate stories based on given prompts or themes. By providing an initial story idea or plot outline, users can engage in a collaborative storytelling process with ChatGPT. The model can continue the story, introduce new characters, or develop plot twists, contributing to the creative writing process.
2. Character Development: ChatGPT can assist in character development by providing descriptions, background information, or personality traits for fictional characters. Users can ask questions about their characters or seek suggestions for their unique attributes, helping to shape and refine the creative elements of the story.
3. Setting Descriptions: ChatGPT can generate vivid descriptions of settings or locations within a story. Users can request detailed portrayals of landscapes, cities, or imaginary realms, enhancing the visual imagery and immersiveness of the storytelling process.
4. Creative Ideas and Inspiration: ChatGPT can offer creative ideas and inspiration for writing projects. Users can seek suggestions for plot twists, dialogue lines, or unique story concepts. ChatGPT's generative capabilities can stimulate creativity and help overcome writer's block.
5. Collaborative Writing: Users can engage in collaborative writing with ChatGPT by alternating turns in writing paragraphs or sections of a story. ChatGPT can respond to

user contributions, expanding upon them and maintaining the continuity of the narrative. This collaborative approach can foster creativity and generate unique storylines.

6. Writing Prompts and Exercises: ChatGPT can provide writing prompts or exercises to inspire creative writing endeavors. Users can request specific types of prompts, such as mystery, romance, or science fiction, to generate ideas and kickstart their writing process.

7. Style and Tone Exploration: ChatGPT can assist in exploring different writing styles or tones. Users can experiment with various styles by asking ChatGPT to generate text in specific voices or mimic the writing styles of famous authors. This exploration can contribute to honing writing skills and discovering new creative approaches.

While ChatGPT can be a valuable tool for creative writing and storytelling, it's important to remember that the generated content should be critically evaluated and refined by the user. ChatGPT's suggestions and contributions serve as creative prompts or inspiration, but the final creative decisions and editing should come from the writer.

OpenAI encourages users to experiment with ChatGPT's creative writing capabilities and provide feedback to improve its performance and ensure a more engaging and interactive experience in the realm of creative writing and storytelling.

GENERATING CODE AND TECHNICAL CONTENT

ChatGPT can be used to assist with generating code snippets and technical content, providing helpful suggestions and information in various programming and technical domains. Here's how ChatGPT can be utilized for generating code and technical content:

1. Code Snippet Generation: ChatGPT can generate code snippets based on user queries or specific programming tasks. By describing the desired functionality or providing relevant context, users can request code examples that demonstrate how to solve particular programming problems or implement specific functionalities.
2. Language Syntax and Usage: ChatGPT can provide guidance on programming language syntax, usage, and best practices. Users can ask questions about specific language constructs, library functions, or coding patterns, and ChatGPT can generate explanations, code samples, or references to relevant documentation.
3. Troubleshooting and Debugging Assistance: Users can seek assistance from ChatGPT when troubleshooting code errors or debugging issues. By describing the problem or error message, users can ask for suggestions on possible solutions or approaches to resolve the coding problem at hand.
4. Documentation Generation: ChatGPT can assist in generating technical documentation or explanations. Users can provide descriptions of a particular functionality, API, or software component, and ChatGPT can generate detailed documentation or explanations in a format suitable for technical writing.

5. Algorithm Explanations: ChatGPT can provide explanations and descriptions of various algorithms used in programming and computer science. Users can request explanations of sorting algorithms, graph algorithms, or other computational concepts, and ChatGPT can generate informative descriptions and code examples.

6. Programming Paradigm Insights: ChatGPT can offer insights and explanations on different programming paradigms, design patterns, or architectural concepts. Users can inquire about object-oriented programming, functional programming, or other software engineering concepts, and ChatGPT can provide relevant explanations and examples.

7. API Usage and Integration: ChatGPT can assist in understanding and utilizing various APIs and software libraries. Users can ask questions about integrating specific APIs into their projects or how to make effective use of certain functionalities, and ChatGPT can provide guidance and code snippets to aid in the integration process.

It's important to note that while ChatGPT can generate code snippets and technical content, users should verify and review the generated code for correctness and adherence to coding standards. Additionally, caution should be exercised when using the generated code in production environments, as thorough testing and validation are necessary.

OpenAI encourages users to provide feedback and engage in responsible use of ChatGPT for generating code and technical content, helping to improve the system's capabilities and ensure accurate and useful outputs in the programming and technical domains.

ETHICAL CONSIDERATIONS

Ethical considerations play a crucial role in the development and use of AI systems like ChatGPT. OpenAI acknowledges the importance of responsible AI development and promotes ethical guidelines to ensure the appropriate and beneficial use of their technology. Here are some key ethical considerations related to ChatGPT:

1. Bias and Fairness: ChatGPT's training data can contain biases present in the source text it learns from. Efforts are made to mitigate biases during data collection and fine-tuning processes. However, it's crucial to remain vigilant in identifying and addressing any biases that may emerge in the system's responses to ensure fairness and inclusivity.

2. Harmful or Misleading Content: Measures are taken to avoid generating content that is harmful, malicious, or misleading. OpenAI implements filtering and moderation mechanisms to reduce the risk of ChatGPT producing inappropriate or false information. However, no system is perfect, and user feedback is vital in identifying and rectifying any potential issues.

3. User Consent and Privacy: OpenAI respects user privacy and emphasizes the importance of obtaining user consent for data usage. ChatGPT interactions may be logged to improve the system, but efforts are made to handle data securely and protect user privacy.

4. Responsible Use and Guidelines: OpenAI provides guidelines to users on the responsible and appropriate use of ChatGPT. Users are encouraged to avoid malicious activities, impersonation, harassment, or generating harmful content. Understanding and adhering to these guidelines helps ensure the ethical use of ChatGPT.

5. Transparency and Explainability: OpenAI aims to improve the transparency and explainability of AI systems like ChatGPT. Efforts are made to provide clearer explanations of how the system works, its limitations, and potential biases. This transparency helps users understand the system's capabilities and make informed decisions.
6. Feedback and Iterative Improvement: OpenAI actively seeks user feedback to address limitations, improve system behavior, and mitigate ethical concerns. User feedback helps identify and rectify issues, refine the system's behavior, and make it more aligned with user expectations.

Ethical considerations are an ongoing focus for OpenAI, and they actively work to improve ChatGPT's behavior and address emerging challenges. OpenAI encourages collaboration with the wider community to ensure a collective effort in upholding ethical standards and creating AI systems that benefit society as a whole.

By considering these ethical considerations and engaging in responsible use, users can contribute to the development of AI systems like ChatGPT in a manner that aligns with ethical principles and societal well-being.

BIAS AND FAIRNESS IN LANGUAGE MODELS

Bias and fairness in language models, including ChatGPT, are important considerations in AI development. Here are some key points regarding bias and fairness in language models:

1. Data Bias: Language models like ChatGPT learn from large text datasets, which can inadvertently contain biases present in the data sources. Biases can stem from societal, cultural, or historical factors reflected in the training data. These biases may manifest in the model's responses and have the potential to perpetuate stereotypes or discrimination.

2. Mitigating Bias: OpenAI recognizes the importance of mitigating biases in language models. Efforts are made to carefully curate and preprocess training data, filter out biased sources, and minimize the amplification of biases during training. Ongoing research focuses on developing techniques to reduce biases and improve fairness in language models.

3. Bias Identification and Evaluation: OpenAI actively evaluates language models for biases, both pre-release and during operation. They conduct rigorous testing and analysis to identify and rectify biases that may emerge in the system's responses. User feedback is invaluable in identifying biases and addressing them effectively.

4. User Feedback and Iterative Improvement: OpenAI encourages users to provide feedback when they encounter biased or unfair outputs from ChatGPT. User feedback helps in understanding and addressing biases, improving system behavior, and enhancing fairness. It plays a vital role in the iterative improvement of language models.

5. Fairness in System Outputs: OpenAI aims to ensure that language models like ChatGPT provide fair and equitable responses to all users. Efforts are made to treat users impartially, regardless of their background, race, gender, or other protected characteristics. OpenAI strives to improve the fairness and inclusivity of the system's outputs.
6. User Customization and Control: OpenAI is actively working on developing an upgrade to ChatGPT that allows users to customize its behavior within certain limits. This approach aims to empower users to define their AI's values and ensure that the system aligns better with their preferences, thereby addressing biases and personalizing the AI experience.

Addressing bias and promoting fairness in language models is an ongoing area of research and development. OpenAI is committed to transparency, accountability, and continuous improvement to ensure that language models are built with fairness and ethical considerations in mind.

It's important for developers, researchers, and users to collectively work towards identifying and mitigating biases in language models, creating systems that respect diversity, inclusivity, and fairness in their responses and behavior.

RESPONSIBLE USE OF CHATGPT

Responsible use of ChatGPT is essential to ensure its ethical and beneficial deployment. Here are some guidelines for the responsible use of ChatGPT:

1. Understand its Limitations: Recognize that ChatGPT is an AI model and has limitations. It may generate incorrect, biased, or nonsensical responses. Be aware of these limitations and exercise critical judgment when interpreting and using the generated content.
2. Contextual Awareness: Provide clear and specific instructions or prompts to help ChatGPT understand the desired context and generate more accurate responses. Clearly communicate your intentions and expectations to obtain relevant and meaningful outputs.
3. Verify and Fact-Check: Independently verify and fact-check the information or responses generated by ChatGPT, especially when it comes to important or sensitive matters. Do not solely rely on ChatGPT's output as the sole source of truth.
4. Avoid Malicious Use: Do not engage in activities that may cause harm, violate ethical standards, or promote malicious intent. Refrain from using ChatGPT to generate content that is defamatory, offensive, or deceptive.
5. Protect Privacy and Confidentiality: Avoid sharing sensitive or personally identifiable information during interactions with ChatGPT. Be cautious when discussing personal, confidential, or sensitive matters, as AI systems may not guarantee complete privacy or data security.
6. Provide Feedback: Share feedback with OpenAI when encountering issues, biases, or other concerns with ChatGPT. User feedback is invaluable in identifying and

improving system behavior, addressing biases, and enhancing its overall performance.
7. Follow OpenAI Guidelines: Adhere to OpenAI's guidelines and terms of service while using ChatGPT. Familiarize yourself with their recommendations and policies to ensure responsible and compliant usage.
8. Promote Ethical Applications: Encourage the responsible and ethical application of AI technologies. Share knowledge, guidelines, and best practices with others to foster a culture of responsible AI use and ensure its positive impact on society.

OpenAI actively seeks to address concerns, improve system behavior, and refine ChatGPT based on user feedback and ongoing research. By responsibly using and providing feedback on ChatGPT, users can contribute to the development of AI systems that align with ethical standards and benefit the broader community.

PRIVACY AND SECURITY CONCERNS

Privacy and security concerns are important considerations when using AI systems like ChatGPT. Here are some points to address privacy and security concerns:

1. Data Handling: OpenAI takes measures to handle user data responsibly. While ChatGPT interactions may be logged for improving the system, OpenAI emphasizes the protection of user privacy. Familiarize yourself with OpenAI's data usage policies and ensure that you are comfortable with the information you share during interactions.
2. Personal and Sensitive Information: Avoid sharing personal, sensitive, or confidential information during interactions with ChatGPT. Be cautious when discussing topics that involve personally identifiable details, financial data, passwords, or any sensitive information that could compromise your privacy or security.
3. User Responsibility: Users have a role in protecting their own privacy and security. Exercise caution and avoid sharing unnecessary personal details or sensitive information that is not required for the interaction with ChatGPT. Treat AI interactions with the same level of discretion as any other online interaction.
4. Secure Communication Channels: Ensure that you are interacting with ChatGPT through secure and trusted channels. Use official and reputable platforms or interfaces provided by OpenAI to minimize the risk of unauthorized access or data breaches.
5. Encryption and Data Security: When interacting with ChatGPT, ensure that your connection is encrypted, particularly when transmitting sensitive information. Use secure and up-to-date communication protocols and

platforms to maintain the confidentiality and integrity of your data.
6. Responsible AI Usage: As a user, it's important to be mindful of the content generated by ChatGPT. Avoid using AI systems for malicious purposes, spreading misinformation, or engaging in harmful activities that may compromise privacy, security, or ethical standards.
7. Feedback and Reporting: If you encounter any privacy or security issues or suspect potential vulnerabilities, promptly report them to OpenAI. By sharing feedback on privacy and security concerns, you contribute to the improvement of AI systems and help maintain a secure and trustworthy environment.

OpenAI acknowledges the importance of privacy and security and continually works to address these concerns. By understanding and following best practices, users can mitigate privacy and security risks associated with AI interactions, promoting a safer and more secure user experience.

MITIGATING POTENTIAL RISKS

Mitigating potential risks associated with AI systems like ChatGPT is crucial for responsible and safe usage. Here are some measures to consider when using ChatGPT:

1. User Awareness and Education: Users should be aware of the capabilities, limitations, and potential risks associated with AI systems like ChatGPT. Educate yourself about the technology, its applications, and the responsible use guidelines to make informed decisions.
2. Critical Evaluation: Exercise critical thinking and evaluate the outputs generated by ChatGPT. Do not blindly trust or rely solely on the system's responses. Verify information independently and consider multiple sources to ensure accuracy and avoid potential misinformation.
3. Contextual Input: Provide clear and specific instructions or prompts to help ChatGPT understand the desired context. Clearly communicate your intent and expectations to obtain more accurate and relevant responses.
4. Monitoring and Feedback: Continuously monitor the responses generated by ChatGPT during interactions. Provide feedback to OpenAI if you encounter issues, biases, or concerns. User feedback plays a crucial role in identifying and rectifying potential risks and improving the system's behavior.
5. Responsible Use: Adhere to OpenAI's guidelines and terms of service when using ChatGPT. Avoid engaging in malicious activities, spreading misinformation, or using the technology in ways that may harm others or violate ethical standards.
6. Privacy Protection: Be mindful of the personal and sensitive information you share during interactions with ChatGPT.

Avoid disclosing unnecessary personal details or sensitive data that could compromise your privacy or security. Familiarize yourself with OpenAI's data usage policies to understand how your information is handled.

7. Secure Communication: Ensure that you interact with ChatGPT through secure and trusted channels. Use official interfaces and platforms provided by OpenAI to minimize the risk of unauthorized access or data breaches.

8. Ongoing Improvements: OpenAI is actively working on improving ChatGPT and addressing potential risks. Stay updated with system updates and improvements to benefit from enhanced safety measures and advancements in the technology.

By being proactive, vigilant, and responsible users, we can collectively contribute to mitigating potential risks associated with AI systems like ChatGPT. Responsible usage and continuous feedback help ensure the development and deployment of AI technologies that prioritize safety, reliability, and user well-being.

CONVERSATIONS WITH CHATGPT

Engaging in conversations with ChatGPT can be a dynamic and interactive experience. Here are some tips for having effective and engaging conversations:

1. Clear and Specific Prompts: Provide clear and specific prompts or questions to help ChatGPT understand your intent. Well-formulated prompts increase the likelihood of receiving relevant and accurate responses.
2. Contextual Information: When continuing a conversation, provide necessary context from previous exchanges to help ChatGPT maintain continuity and better understand the ongoing dialogue. Refer back to specific points or ask ChatGPT to recall previous information if needed.
3. Ask for Clarification: If a response from ChatGPT is unclear or requires further elaboration, don't hesitate to ask for clarification. Request specific details or examples to enhance the clarity of the conversation.
4. Be Patient: ChatGPT may take a moment to generate responses, especially for more complex queries. Be patient while waiting for the system to generate a thoughtful and relevant response. It's also important to be patient if ChatGPT occasionally produces incorrect or nonsensical answers.
5. Guide the Conversation: Guide the conversation by providing more specific instructions or narrowing down the topic. You can request opinions, compare options, or ask for pros and cons to facilitate a more focused discussion.
6. Experiment and Explore: Feel free to experiment with different types of questions, writing styles, or tones to see how ChatGPT responds. You can explore creative scenarios, engage in role-play, or test the system's knowledge in

various domains. Remember to critically evaluate the generated content and use it as a source of inspiration rather than absolute truth.

7. Provide Feedback: If you notice any issues, biases, or areas for improvement during your conversation, provide feedback to OpenAI. Your feedback helps in refining the system and addressing potential limitations or concerns.

Remember that while ChatGPT strives to generate accurate and helpful responses, it has limitations and may occasionally produce incorrect or nonsensical answers. Use your judgment, verify information independently, and take responsibility for interpreting and applying the generated content appropriately.

Engaging in conversations with ChatGPT can be an opportunity for exploration, learning, and creativity. By providing clear instructions, offering context, and actively participating in the dialogue, you can have more meaningful and engaging interactions with ChatGPT.

INTERACTION EXAMPLES AND USE CASES

ChatGPT can be used in various scenarios to facilitate interactive and informative conversations. Here are some interaction examples and use cases for ChatGPT:

1. Information and Knowledge Sharing:
   - User: "What is the capital of France?"
   - ChatGPT: "The capital of France is Paris."
2. Creative Writing Assistance:
   - User: "Can you help me come up with a catchy opening line for a novel?"
   - ChatGPT: "Sure! What genre is your novel? Any specific themes or tone you'd like to convey?"
3. Learning and Education:
   - User: "Can you explain the concept of quantum entanglement?"
   - ChatGPT: "Quantum entanglement is a phenomenon in which two or more particles become interconnected..."
4. Problem Solving and Programming Help:
   - User: "I'm getting a 'SyntaxError' in my Python code. What could be the issue?"
   - ChatGPT: "Syntax errors typically occur when there's a mistake in the structure or formatting of your code..."
5. Content Generation:
   - User: "Can you help me write a product description for a new smartphone?"
   - ChatGPT: "Of course! What are the key features and selling points of the smartphone?"
6. Decision Making and Recommendations:

- o User: "I'm planning a vacation. Can you suggest some popular destinations in Europe?"
  - o ChatGPT: "Certainly! What are your preferences in terms of activities, budget, and travel dates?"
7. Exploring Historical Events:
  - o User: "Tell me more about the Apollo 11 moon landing in 1969."
  - o ChatGPT: "The Apollo 11 mission was the first crewed mission to land on the moon..."
8. Role-Playing and Interactive Storytelling:
  - o User: "Let's create a fantasy story together. You start!"
  - o ChatGPT: "Once upon a time, in the enchanted land of..." [The user and ChatGPT take turns expanding the story.]

These examples demonstrate some of the diverse ways in which ChatGPT can be utilized for interactive and engaging conversations. From answering factual queries to assisting with creative writing, learning, decision-making, and storytelling, ChatGPT offers a wide range of applications.

Keep in mind that while ChatGPT strives to provide accurate and helpful responses, it has limitations and may occasionally produce incorrect or nonsensical answers. Use your discretion, critically evaluate the generated content, and ensure responsible use of the technology.

CHATGPT AS A CONVERSATIONAL AGENT

ChatGPT serves as a conversational agent, engaging users in interactive and dynamic conversations. As a conversational agent, ChatGPT exhibits the following characteristics:

1. Natural Language Understanding: ChatGPT can comprehend and interpret natural language inputs from users, allowing for seamless and human-like conversations. It understands user queries, prompts, and instructions to generate relevant responses.
2. Contextual Responses: ChatGPT takes into account the conversation history and context to generate contextually appropriate responses. It can reference previous user inputs and maintain a basic memory of the ongoing dialogue, contributing to a more coherent and meaningful conversation flow.
3. Language Generation: ChatGPT excels at generating human-like text responses. It leverages its training on vast amounts of data to produce coherent, grammatically correct, and contextually relevant answers. Its language generation capabilities enable dynamic and engaging interactions.
4. Multi-Turn Dialogue: ChatGPT is designed to handle multi-turn conversations, allowing for back-and-forth exchanges with users. It maintains context and generates responses based on the evolving conversation, facilitating interactive and continuous dialogue.
5. Knowledge and Information Sharing: ChatGPT possesses a broad understanding of general knowledge and can provide information, explanations, and insights on various topics. Users can ask questions, seek explanations, or request details, and ChatGPT responds with relevant information.

6. Personalization and Adaptability: ChatGPT can adapt its language style, tone, or level of formality based on user prompts. It can mimic certain personas, adjust its responses to specific preferences, or align with the desired communication style, providing a more personalized conversational experience.

7. Assistance and Recommendations: ChatGPT can offer assistance, suggestions, and recommendations in diverse domains. It can provide guidance, propose ideas, offer solutions, or make relevant recommendations based on user queries or needs.

8. Continuous Improvement: OpenAI actively seeks user feedback to improve the performance and behavior of ChatGPT as a conversational agent. Feedback helps in identifying areas for refinement, addressing limitations, and ensuring that ChatGPT evolves to meet user expectations and needs.

ChatGPT's conversational agent capabilities make it a versatile tool for interactive discussions, information retrieval, content generation, and assistance across various domains. Users can engage with ChatGPT as a virtual assistant, a knowledge resource, or a partner in creative endeavors, benefiting from its conversational and language understanding abilities.

PERSONALIZING AND CUSTOMIZING CHATGPT'S BEHAVIOR

Personalizing and customizing ChatGPT's behavior is an area of active development by OpenAI. While customization options are not currently available in the base version of ChatGPT, OpenAI is working on an upgrade that allows users to have more control over the system's behavior. Here are some aspects of personalization and customization that OpenAI is exploring:

1. User Preferences: OpenAI aims to develop features that allow users to specify their preferences and values to shape ChatGPT's responses. This would enable users to customize the system's behavior according to their individual needs and preferences.
2. Style and Tone: OpenAI is working on providing users with the ability to adjust ChatGPT's language style, formality, or tone. Users may be able to choose between different writing styles, such as casual or professional, to align with the intended context.
3. Content Filtering: OpenAI recognizes the importance of content filtering to ensure appropriate and safe interactions. They are actively researching ways to enable users to define and set limits on the types of content ChatGPT generates, thereby ensuring compliance with their preferences and requirements.
4. Ethical Guidelines: OpenAI is considering methods to allow users to customize ChatGPT's behavior within certain ethical boundaries. While the specifics are still being developed, the goal is to provide users with tools to ensure responsible and ethical use of the technology.

These personalization and customization features are intended to empower users to tailor ChatGPT's behavior to their specific needs while maintaining ethical standards and preventing misuse. OpenAI is actively seeking user input and feedback to shape the customization capabilities and ensure they align with user expectations.

It's important to note that striking the right balance between customization and ethical considerations is a complex task. OpenAI is committed to addressing challenges and ensuring that customization options empower users while also upholding fairness, safety, and responsible AI use.

As developments progress, users can look forward to more opportunities to personalize and customize ChatGPT's behavior to enhance its utility and align it with individual requirements.

FUTURE OF CHATGPT AND BEYOND

The future of ChatGPT holds exciting possibilities as OpenAI continues to advance the technology and address its limitations. Here are some potential directions and advancements for ChatGPT and AI systems:

1. Enhanced Language Understanding: OpenAI aims to improve ChatGPT's language understanding capabilities, enabling it to comprehend user inputs more accurately and handle complex queries with greater proficiency. This advancement would lead to more precise and contextually aware responses.
2. Customization and Control: OpenAI is working on developing features that allow users to customize ChatGPT's behavior and responses within predefined ethical boundaries. This customization would enable users to tailor the system to their specific needs, promoting a more personalized and satisfactory user experience.
3. Multimodal Capabilities: OpenAI is exploring the integration of visual and audio inputs into ChatGPT, enabling it to process and generate responses based on a combination of text, images, and audio. This would expand its applications to domains that require multimodal understanding, such as image description or voice-based interactions.
4. Improved Responsiveness and Speed: OpenAI is actively working on reducing the response times of ChatGPT, allowing for more natural and dynamic conversational exchanges. Faster response generation would enhance the interactive nature of conversations with ChatGPT.
5. Collaboration and Cooperation: OpenAI envisions AI systems like ChatGPT being able to collaborate with humans and other AI systems effectively. This collaborative

capability could foster cooperative problem-solving, creative endeavors, and collective intelligence, leading to more impactful and efficient outcomes.

6. Ethical Advancements: OpenAI remains committed to addressing biases, ensuring fairness, and addressing ethical concerns associated with AI systems. Ongoing research and development focus on enhancing system transparency, explainability, and accountability to create AI technologies that benefit all users and society as a whole.

7. User Feedback and Iterative Improvement: OpenAI values user feedback and considers it instrumental in refining and advancing ChatGPT. Continuous user engagement and feedback help identify limitations, biases, and potential areas for improvement, driving iterative updates and enhancing the system's performance.

As AI technology progresses, ChatGPT and similar systems will continue to evolve, becoming more capable, versatile, and user-centric. OpenAI strives to create AI systems that are valuable, trustworthy, and aligned with user needs, while also upholding ethical standards and addressing societal considerations.

The future of ChatGPT and AI systems holds immense potential to transform various domains, including communication, creativity, education, problem-solving, and more. With ongoing research, development, and user collaboration, ChatGPT is poised to become an increasingly powerful and beneficial tool for users worldwide.

RECENT ADVANCEMENTS AND RESEARCH IN LANGUAGE MODELS

Recent advancements and research in language models have witnessed notable progress in various areas. Here are some key highlights:

1. Pretraining Techniques: Researchers have explored advanced pretraining methods to improve language models. Techniques like self-supervised learning, unsupervised fine-tuning, and self-training have been investigated to enhance model performance and reduce the need for extensive labeled data.
2. Multimodal Models: The integration of vision and language has gained attention. Multimodal models combine text with images or videos to enable understanding, generation, and reasoning across different modalities. This research area aims to develop models that can comprehend and generate content based on both textual and visual information.
3. Few-Shot and Zero-Shot Learning: Efforts have been made to enhance models' ability to learn from limited or even zero examples in a specific task or domain. Techniques like meta-learning, transfer learning, and zero-shot learning enable models to generalize knowledge and adapt to new tasks with minimal training data.
4. Bias Mitigation: Addressing biases in language models has been a focus of research. Techniques aim to reduce the amplification of biases present in training data and to develop fairer, more unbiased models. Methods such as dataset curation, fine-tuning procedures, and bias measurement metrics have been explored to promote fairness and mitigate biases.

5. Explainability and Interpretability: Researchers are working towards improving the interpretability and explainability of language models. Techniques aim to provide insights into the model's decision-making process, understand the model's reasoning, and identify factors that influence its outputs. This research helps enhance transparency and accountability in AI systems.

6. Efficient and Lightweight Models: Development of more efficient and lightweight language models has been a focus. Researchers aim to reduce computational resource requirements and model size while maintaining performance. Techniques like knowledge distillation, model compression, and architecture design modifications contribute to the development of more efficient models.

7. Multilingual and Cross-lingual Models: Research has focused on building language models that can understand and generate content in multiple languages. Multilingual and cross-lingual models aim to facilitate communication, translation, and understanding across diverse linguistic contexts, enabling more inclusive and globally applicable AI systems.

These advancements and ongoing research efforts contribute to the evolution and improvement of language models. They address various challenges, enhance model capabilities, and drive progress in areas such as bias mitigation, multimodal understanding, interpretability, efficiency, and cross-lingual capabilities.

It's important to note that the field of language models is continuously evolving, and new research breakthroughs emerge regularly. These advancements pave the way for more sophisticated and powerful language models that can better serve diverse applications and user needs.

OPENAI'S ROADMAP FOR CHATGPT

OpenAI has outlined a roadmap for the development and enhancement of ChatGPT. While specific details and timelines may evolve, the roadmap highlights OpenAI's strategic directions and goals. Here are the key elements of OpenAI's roadmap for ChatGPT:

1. Improving Default Behavior: OpenAI aims to enhance ChatGPT's default behavior to make it more useful and aligned with user expectations. This involves reducing both obvious and subtle biases, addressing limitations, and refining the system's responses to provide more accurate and reliable information.
2. Customization: OpenAI is developing an upgrade to ChatGPT that allows users to customize its behavior while ensuring ethical boundaries are respected. This feature will empower users to define their AI's values and preferences within certain limits, enabling a more personalized and tailored user experience.
3. Public Input: OpenAI recognizes the importance of involving the public in decisions about system behavior, defaults, and deployment policies. They seek external input, including public consultations, to gather diverse perspectives and shape the development and deployment of ChatGPT in a way that aligns with societal values.
4. Expanded Offerings: OpenAI plans to provide additional offerings of ChatGPT to cater to a broader range of user needs. These may include variations in the model's behavior, capabilities, and pricing options, aiming to meet the specific requirements of different user groups and use cases.

5. Partnerships and Integration: OpenAI intends to collaborate with external organizations and partners to integrate ChatGPT into various applications, services, and platforms. By working with other developers and industry experts, OpenAI aims to unlock the potential of ChatGPT in diverse domains and make it more widely accessible.

OpenAI's roadmap for ChatGPT reflects their commitment to continuous improvement, responsible development, and user feedback. The focus on enhancing default behavior, enabling customization, incorporating public input, expanding offerings, and fostering partnerships highlights OpenAI's dedication to creating AI systems that are valuable, trustworthy, and aligned with user needs and societal values.

As the roadmap unfolds, OpenAI welcomes user feedback and external input to ensure that ChatGPT's development remains transparent, accountable, and serves the best interests of the wider community.

POTENTIAL APPLICATIONS AND IMPACT IN VARIOUS INDUSTRIES

ChatGPT has the potential to impact various industries and domains by offering versatile and interactive conversational capabilities. Here are some potential applications and impacts of ChatGPT in different industries:

1. Customer Service and Support: ChatGPT can assist with customer inquiries, providing personalized and responsive support. It can handle common queries, offer troubleshooting guidance, and provide information about products and services, improving customer satisfaction and reducing support costs.
2. E-commerce and Sales: ChatGPT can act as a virtual shopping assistant, helping users find products, recommend alternatives, and answer questions about features or specifications. Its conversational abilities can enhance the online shopping experience and drive sales conversion.
3. Content Creation and Writing: ChatGPT can assist with content generation, offering ideas, suggestions, and even drafting written material. It can be utilized by content creators, copywriters, and marketers to enhance productivity and creativity in writing tasks.
4. Education and E-Learning: ChatGPT can support students and learners by providing explanations, answering questions, and offering educational resources. It can act as a virtual tutor or mentor, fostering personalized learning experiences and expanding access to educational materials.
5. Healthcare and Medical Support: ChatGPT can assist in providing basic medical information, answering non-emergency health-related queries, and offering guidance

on healthy living practices. It can serve as a reliable source of information, complementing healthcare providers' services.

6. Information Retrieval and Knowledge Management: ChatGPT can aid in retrieving information from vast repositories, databases, or knowledge bases. It can assist researchers, professionals, and individuals in accessing relevant information quickly and accurately.

7. Human Resources and Recruitment: ChatGPT can support HR departments in handling routine inquiries, assisting with onboarding processes, and providing information about company policies. It can streamline recruitment processes by answering candidate questions and offering initial screening.

8. Virtual Assistants and Personal Productivity: ChatGPT can act as a virtual assistant, helping users with scheduling, reminders, task management, and general productivity support. It can provide personalized recommendations and suggestions to enhance individual efficiency and time management.

9. Gaming and Entertainment: ChatGPT can contribute to interactive and immersive gaming experiences by providing intelligent in-game characters, dialogue systems, and natural language interfaces. It can enhance storytelling, offer hints or guidance, and adapt the game based on user interactions.

10. Social and Community Platforms: ChatGPT can be integrated into social platforms to facilitate engaging conversations, provide recommendations, and enhance user interactions. It can contribute to community engagement, content moderation, and user support on online platforms.

These are just a few examples of how ChatGPT can impact various industries. Its conversational capabilities, knowledge dissemination, and personalized interactions have the potential to revolutionize the way we interact with technology and enhance user experiences across diverse sectors.

BUILDING YOUR OWN CHATBOT WITH CHATGPT

Building your own chatbot using ChatGPT involves integrating the ChatGPT API into your application or platform. Here's a high-level overview of the process:

1. Obtain API Access: Sign up for the OpenAI API and obtain the necessary access credentials, such as an API key or authentication tokens. This will allow your application to interact with ChatGPT.
2. API Integration: Implement the API integration in your application or platform. This involves making HTTP requests to the ChatGPT API endpoint, passing your API credentials, and providing the desired user prompts or messages for generating responses.
3. User Interface: Design and develop a user interface that enables users to interact with the chatbot. This can be a web-based interface, a mobile app, a messaging platform, or any other interface that suits your application's requirements.
4. Input Processing: Preprocess and format user inputs to ensure they are in a suitable format for the ChatGPT API. You may need to handle user prompts, handle multi-turn conversations, or incorporate user-specific context into the conversation flow.
5. Make API Requests: Send requests to the ChatGPT API endpoint, providing the user prompts or messages as input. Receive the API responses, which will contain the generated chatbot responses based on the given inputs.
6. Response Handling: Process the API responses and display them to the user through the user interface. You can customize the way responses are presented, format them

appropriately, and handle any additional actions or
functionalities based on the received responses.
7. Iterative Improvement: Continuously gather user feedback,
   monitor the chatbot's performance, and iterate on the
   design and functionality. This will help you refine the
   chatbot's behavior, address limitations, and enhance the
   user experience.

It's important to consider the ethical implications, privacy considerations, and potential biases in your chatbot's implementation. Ensure responsible use, handle user data securely, and actively monitor and address any biases or issues that may arise during interactions.

OpenAI provides detailed API documentation, guides, and code examples to assist developers in integrating ChatGPT into their applications. Make sure to refer to the official OpenAI documentation for comprehensive instructions and best practices during the development process.

OVERVIEW OF CHATBOT DEVELOPMENT

Developing a chatbot involves several key steps to create an interactive conversational system. Here's a general overview of the chatbot development process:

1. Define Objectives and Use Cases: Determine the purpose and goals of your chatbot. Identify the specific tasks, functions, or services it will provide. Consider the target audience and the problems the chatbot aims to solve.
2. Choose a Development Approach: Decide whether to build a rule-based chatbot or an AI-powered chatbot. Rule-based chatbots follow predefined rules and patterns, while AI-powered chatbots leverage machine learning techniques for natural language understanding and generation.
3. Data Collection and Preparation: If building an AI-powered chatbot, collect and preprocess relevant data. This may involve gathering conversational datasets, cleaning and formatting the data, and preparing it for training the chatbot model.
4. Select a Development Framework or Platform: Choose a chatbot development framework or platform that suits your requirements. Popular options include frameworks like Microsoft Bot Framework, Dialogflow, or custom development using programming languages like Python.
5. Design Conversation Flows: Define the conversation flow and user interactions. Plan the structure of dialogues, including intents, entities, and possible user responses. Design a user-friendly and intuitive conversational experience.
6. Implement Natural Language Processing (NLP): If using an AI-powered chatbot, integrate NLP capabilities. This involves leveraging NLP libraries, APIs, or services to

perform tasks like intent recognition, entity extraction, and sentiment analysis to understand user inputs.

7. Develop Response Generation: Create mechanisms to generate appropriate responses based on user inputs. This can involve rule-based matching, using predefined response templates, or leveraging machine learning techniques to generate contextually relevant and coherent responses.

8. Integration and Deployment: Integrate the chatbot into the desired platform or application. Deploy the chatbot to a web server, cloud service, or messaging platforms like Facebook Messenger or Slack. Ensure proper connectivity and handle user authentication if required.

9. Testing and Iterative Improvement: Thoroughly test the chatbot's functionality, performance, and user experience. Collect feedback from users and make iterative improvements based on their interactions and suggestions. Continuously monitor and update the chatbot to enhance its capabilities.

10. Maintenance and Updates: Regularly maintain and update the chatbot to ensure it remains functional, up-to-date, and aligned with user needs. Monitor usage patterns, address any issues, and keep the chatbot's knowledge base or AI model updated.

Throughout the development process, consider privacy and security concerns, ensure responsible use of data, and address potential biases in the chatbot's responses. Regularly evaluate and refine the chatbot's performance based on user feedback and evolving requirements.

Remember that chatbot development is an ongoing process, and improvements can be made over time. Stay updated with the latest advancements in chatbot technologies and techniques to deliver a more effective and engaging conversational experience.

IMPLEMENTING CHATGPT IN YOUR OWN PROJECTS

Implementing ChatGPT in your own projects involves utilizing the OpenAI API to integrate ChatGPT's capabilities into your application. Here's a general guide on how to implement ChatGPT:

1. Sign up for OpenAI API: Register and obtain access to the OpenAI API. Follow the instructions provided by OpenAI to get the necessary API credentials, such as an API key or authentication tokens.
2. Familiarize Yourself with the API: Review the API documentation provided by OpenAI. Understand the available endpoints, request formats, and response structures. Pay attention to any usage limits or guidelines outlined by OpenAI.
3. Set Up API Integration: Choose a programming language or framework for your project. Utilize the appropriate HTTP client libraries to interact with the OpenAI API. Make sure you have the necessary dependencies and tools installed.
4. Authentication and Authorization: Incorporate your API credentials (API key or authentication tokens) into your application's code to authenticate API requests. This typically involves adding the credentials to the HTTP headers of your API requests.
5. Construct API Requests: Create API requests to interact with ChatGPT. Formulate requests that include user prompts or messages as input for generating responses. Specify parameters like the model variant (e.g., "davinci" or "curie") and desired system behavior if applicable.
6. Handle API Responses: Capture and process the responses received from the ChatGPT API. Extract the generated responses from the API response structure and handle

them appropriately in your application. Format and present the responses to users in a user-friendly manner.

7. Error Handling and Edge Cases: Implement error handling mechanisms to deal with API errors, network issues, and other potential edge cases. Ensure your application gracefully handles errors and provides appropriate feedback to users in case of failures.

8. Test and Iterate: Thoroughly test the integration of ChatGPT in your project. Verify that the responses align with your expectations and desired behavior. Gather user feedback and iterate on the implementation to improve the chatbot's performance and user experience.

9. Monitor and Manage API Usage: Keep track of your API usage, including rate limits and usage quotas. Monitor the consumption of API resources and consider any cost implications based on the OpenAI API pricing model. Optimize your implementation for efficient usage if necessary.

10. Stay Updated: Stay informed about updates, improvements, and any changes to the OpenAI API. Keep an eye on OpenAI's documentation, developer resources, and official announcements to ensure your implementation remains up-to-date and compatible with any API updates.

Remember to adhere to OpenAI's usage policies, terms of service, and guidelines for responsible AI use. Respect data privacy and security considerations when handling user inputs and responses.

By following these steps, you can integrate ChatGPT into your projects and leverage its powerful language generation capabilities to enhance your applications with interactive and intelligent conversational features.

BEST PRACTICES AND TIPS FOR BUILDING EFFECTIVE CHATBOTS

Building effective chatbots involves considering various factors to ensure a seamless and engaging user experience. Here are some best practices and tips to keep in mind when developing chatbots:

1. Define Clear Objectives: Clearly define the purpose and goals of your chatbot. Identify the specific tasks it will perform and the value it will provide to users. Having a clear understanding of your chatbot's objectives helps guide the development process.

2. Understand User Needs: Conduct user research to understand your target audience's needs, preferences, and pain points. Identify common user queries and pain points to design your chatbot's capabilities and responses accordingly.

3. Design Conversational Flows: Plan the conversation flow and user interactions carefully. Define intents, entities, and possible user responses. Ensure the chatbot's dialogue is intuitive, coherent, and user-friendly. Provide clear prompts and instructions to guide users.

4. Use Natural Language Processing (NLP): Incorporate NLP techniques to enable the chatbot to understand user inputs. Implement intent recognition, entity extraction, and sentiment analysis to process and interpret user queries accurately.

5. Provide Personalization: Tailor the chatbot's responses to individual users where possible. Consider user context, preferences, and historical interactions to offer personalized recommendations, suggestions, or responses. Customization enhances the user experience.

6. Balance Automation and Human Support: Determine the appropriate level of automation versus human intervention based on your chatbot's capabilities and the complexity of user queries. Utilize human handover mechanisms when the chatbot reaches its limitations and requires human assistance.
7. Test and Iterate: Regularly test your chatbot's functionality, performance, and user experience. Collect feedback from users and iterate on the design and implementation to address any issues or limitations. Continuous improvement is key to building an effective chatbot.
8. Error Handling and Graceful Failures: Implement error handling mechanisms to gracefully handle unexpected or ambiguous user queries. Clearly communicate when the chatbot is unable to provide a response and provide alternative options or assistance.
9. Maintain a Persona: Define a consistent persona for your chatbot to give it a distinct voice and character. Align the chatbot's tone and language style with your brand or application. A well-defined persona can enhance user engagement and build trust.
10. Privacy and Data Security: Handle user data responsibly and ensure compliance with privacy regulations. Implement encryption, secure storage, and proper data handling practices. Communicate transparently about data usage and obtain user consent when necessary.
11. Monitor and Analyze: Continuously monitor your chatbot's performance and user interactions. Gather analytics and user feedback to understand usage patterns, identify areas for improvement, and enhance the chatbot's capabilities over time.

Remember to keep the user at the center of your chatbot design process. Prioritize user needs, deliver value, and create an enjoyable conversational experience. Regularly update and refine your chatbot based on user feedback and evolving requirements to ensure its effectiveness and relevance.

USER FEEDBACK AND IMPROVING CHATGPT

User feedback plays a crucial role in improving ChatGPT and enhancing its performance. OpenAI actively encourages users to provide feedback to help identify issues, biases, and areas for improvement. Here are some key aspects of user feedback and the process of improving ChatGPT:

1. Soliciting User Feedback: OpenAI actively seeks feedback from users to gather insights and perspectives on ChatGPT's behavior and performance. They provide channels and platforms for users to share their feedback, experiences, and suggestions.
2. Feedback on Outputs: Users can provide feedback on specific outputs generated by ChatGPT. This includes reporting issues such as incorrect or nonsensical responses, biases, or content that may violate OpenAI's usage policies. User feedback helps identify areas that need improvement.
3. Identifying Bias and Unintended Behavior: Users can provide feedback if they observe any biases, offensive content, or problematic behavior in ChatGPT's responses. This feedback is valuable in addressing biases and refining the system to ensure fairness, inclusivity, and ethical considerations.
4. Reporting Novel Risks and Edge Cases: Users are encouraged to report any novel risks or unexpected behavior they encounter while interacting with ChatGPT. This helps OpenAI identify and address potential vulnerabilities, edge cases, or unintended consequences that may arise in real-world usage.
5. Feedback Incorporation: OpenAI analyzes user feedback systematically and uses it to improve ChatGPT's performance. They continuously update and iterate on the

models based on the insights gained from user feedback, helping to refine the system's behavior over time.

6. Responsible Iterative Deployment: OpenAI follows a responsible deployment approach for updates and improvements. They consider the potential impact of changes and carefully evaluate the risks and benefits before deploying new versions or updates to ChatGPT.

7. Addressing Feedback Ethically and Responsibly: OpenAI prioritizes addressing feedback in a way that ensures fairness, transparency, and the alignment of ChatGPT with societal values. They actively work on addressing limitations, reducing biases, and enhancing the system's capabilities based on user input.

OpenAI's commitment to user feedback and iterative improvement demonstrates their dedication to creating AI systems that meet user expectations, adhere to ethical guidelines, and align with societal needs. By actively engaging with users and incorporating their feedback, OpenAI aims to continuously enhance ChatGPT's performance, reliability, and usefulness.

COLLECTING USER FEEDBACK

Collecting user feedback is essential for understanding user experiences, identifying issues, and improving ChatGPT. Here are some strategies for collecting user feedback:

1. Feedback Forms: Provide a feedback form or survey on your website, application, or platform where users can share their thoughts, suggestions, and concerns about their interactions with ChatGPT. Ask specific questions about usability, accuracy, and overall satisfaction.
2. In-App Feedback: Incorporate an in-app feedback feature within your chatbot interface, allowing users to provide feedback directly from the conversation. This can be a dedicated button or command that opens a feedback prompt where users can type and submit their comments.
3. Ratings and Reviews: Encourage users to rate and review their experience with ChatGPT. Consider integrating a rating system or review functionality into your chatbot interface or application. Monitor these ratings and reviews to gain insights into user sentiment and identify areas for improvement.
4. User Surveys: Conduct periodic surveys targeted at users who have interacted with ChatGPT. Ask about their satisfaction level, usability, and specific aspects of their experience. Keep the surveys concise and focused to encourage participation.
5. User Interviews or Focus Groups: Arrange user interviews or conduct focus groups to gain deeper insights into user experiences. Engage with users directly to understand their challenges, expectations, and suggestions. This qualitative feedback can provide valuable insights for improvement.

6. User Analytics: Analyze user interaction data to identify patterns, trends, and usage behaviors. Track metrics such as completion rates, user session durations, and frequently used commands or features. Data-driven insights can help you understand user engagement and areas that require attention.
7. Social Media Listening: Monitor social media platforms, forums, and online communities to listen to user conversations and feedback related to ChatGPT. Look for mentions, hashtags, or discussions around your chatbot to identify user sentiments and address any concerns raised.
8. User Support Channels: Utilize existing user support channels such as customer support emails or chat support to gather feedback. Encourage users to provide feedback regarding their experience with ChatGPT or to report any issues they may have encountered.
9. Beta Testing: Conduct beta testing with a select group of users who can provide early feedback on the chatbot's performance, usability, and overall experience. Encourage them to share their feedback and iterate on the chatbot based on their input before wider deployment.
10. Continuous Engagement: Foster an ongoing dialogue with your user community. Engage in conversations, respond to feedback, and communicate updates or improvements made based on user input. This demonstrates a commitment to user satisfaction and fosters a sense of involvement.

Remember to prioritize user privacy and handle user data securely when collecting feedback. Respect user preferences and provide clear communication about how the feedback will be used and any measures taken to protect user privacy.

By actively seeking and incorporating user feedback, you can gain
valuable insights to improve ChatGPT, enhance its performance,
and deliver a better user experience.

ITERATIVE IMPROVEMENT OF CHATGPT

The iterative improvement of ChatGPT involves an ongoing process of analyzing user feedback, addressing limitations, and refining the model to enhance its performance over time. Here's an overview of the iterative improvement process:

1. User Feedback Collection: OpenAI actively collects user feedback through various channels, including feedback forms, surveys, in-app prompts, and external research partnerships. They encourage users to provide insights, suggestions, and reports on problematic outputs or behavior.
2. Analysis of User Feedback: OpenAI analyzes the collected user feedback to identify common patterns, issues, and areas for improvement. They assess the quality of outputs, understand user needs, and gain insights into potential biases or limitations of the model.
3. Model Updates and Iterations: Based on the analysis of user feedback, OpenAI makes updates and iterations to improve ChatGPT. They fine-tune the model, adjust training processes, and incorporate techniques to address identified issues, reduce biases, and enhance its overall performance.
4. Narrowing Down Failure Modes: OpenAI focuses on narrowing down specific failure modes where ChatGPT produces incorrect or nonsensical outputs. By understanding and addressing these failure modes, they aim to improve the overall reliability and quality of the model's responses.
5. Addressing Bias and Controversial Topics: OpenAI actively works to reduce biases and improve the handling of controversial topics in ChatGPT. They invest in research and

engineering efforts to minimize biased outputs, provide clearer instructions to human reviewers, and refine the fine-tuning process to mitigate potential issues.
6. User Prompts and System Behavior: OpenAI explores ways to allow users to customize ChatGPT's behavior while maintaining ethical boundaries. They aim to provide users with more control over the outputs by incorporating user preferences and values into the generation process.
7. External Input and Audits: OpenAI seeks external input through partnerships, red teaming, and public consultations. They engage with experts, researchers, and the public to obtain diverse perspectives and conduct audits to ensure accountability and transparency in the development and deployment of ChatGPT.
8. Responsible Deployment and Monitoring: OpenAI is committed to responsible deployment of ChatGPT and actively monitors its real-world usage. They continually gather insights, track performance, and make necessary adjustments to ensure the system operates as intended and aligns with societal expectations.

The iterative improvement of ChatGPT is an ongoing process that involves continuous learning, feedback analysis, and updates. OpenAI's goal is to create a more reliable, useful, and safe language model that benefits users while addressing concerns and limitations to the best of their abilities.

CHALLENGES IN USER FEEDBACK AND ADDRESSING THEM

Collecting and addressing user feedback comes with its own set of challenges. Here are some common challenges in user feedback and strategies for addressing them:

1. Limited Quantity: Obtaining a sufficient volume of user feedback can be challenging, especially during the early stages of chatbot deployment. Encourage users to provide feedback through multiple channels, implement in-app prompts, and consider offering incentives to incentivize participation.
2. Biased Subset of Users: The users who provide feedback may not represent the entire user base, leading to a biased sample. To address this, consider reaching out to a diverse group of users, conduct user surveys with targeted questions, and actively seek feedback from underrepresented user segments.
3. Vague or Incomplete Feedback: Users may provide vague or incomplete feedback, making it challenging to understand the underlying issues. Encourage users to provide specific examples, screenshots, or descriptions of their interactions to help you better comprehend and address their concerns.
4. Difficulty in Extracting Actionable Insights: Analyzing and extracting actionable insights from user feedback can be complex, especially when dealing with a large volume of responses. Consider using natural language processing (NLP) techniques to automate sentiment analysis, topic clustering, and keyword extraction to facilitate analysis and identify common themes or issues.

5. Addressing Conflicting Feedback: Users may provide conflicting feedback or have divergent expectations, making it challenging to determine the appropriate course of action. Prioritize feedback based on frequency, severity, or alignment with your chatbot's objectives. Consider conducting user surveys or interviews to gain deeper insights into conflicting feedback and identify potential compromises or alternative solutions.

6. Incorporating Feedback in a Timely Manner: Processing and incorporating user feedback into the chatbot's improvements can be time-consuming. Establish a systematic process for analyzing and prioritizing feedback. Set up regular review cycles to address critical issues and allocate resources accordingly to ensure timely improvements.

7. Balancing User Preferences and Ethical Considerations: User feedback may include requests to customize the chatbot's behavior in ways that may raise ethical concerns or compromise fairness. Strive for a balance between user preferences and ethical guidelines. Consider offering customization options within predefined boundaries to provide users with some control while upholding ethical principles.

8. Communicating Updates to Users: Effectively communicating updates and improvements to users based on their feedback can be challenging. Provide clear and transparent information about the changes made, how user feedback influenced the updates, and the expected impact on the chatbot's behavior. Consider using in-app notifications, release notes, or blog posts to keep users informed.

Addressing these challenges requires a proactive and iterative approach. Actively seek feedback, employ analytical techniques to extract insights, prioritize issues based on their impact, and communicate updates transparently to users. By continuously engaging with users and refining the chatbot based on their feedback, you can improve the overall user experience and build a more effective and valuable chatbot.

THE HUMAN-AI PARTNERSHIP

The human-AI partnership refers to the collaboration and interaction between humans and artificial intelligence systems, working together to achieve mutual goals and enhance overall performance. It recognizes that both humans and AI systems have unique strengths and capabilities that, when combined, can lead to more effective and impactful outcomes. Here are key aspects of the human-AI partnership:

1. Complementary Skills and Capabilities: Humans and AI systems have distinct strengths and weaknesses. Humans excel in areas such as creativity, empathy, and complex reasoning, while AI systems are proficient in data processing, pattern recognition, and scalability. By leveraging their respective strengths, the partnership can accomplish tasks more efficiently and comprehensively.
2. Task Allocation: The human-AI partnership involves assigning tasks to the most suitable agent, whether it is a human or an AI system. Humans can focus on tasks that require critical thinking, judgment, and ethical decision-making, while AI systems can handle repetitive, data-intensive, or computation-heavy tasks. This division of labor maximizes efficiency and optimizes resource utilization.
3. Augmentation and Empowerment: AI systems can augment human capabilities by providing information, insights, and recommendations to support decision-making. Humans can

leverage AI systems to process and analyze vast amounts of data, leading to more informed and data-driven decisions. The partnership empowers humans to make better-informed choices and enables them to focus on higher-level cognitive tasks.

4. Contextual Understanding: Humans bring contextual understanding, common sense reasoning, and domain expertise to the partnership. They can interpret complex nuances, understand social and cultural contexts, and adapt to dynamic situations. AI systems, on the other hand, provide data-driven insights and knowledge across various domains. By combining human understanding with AI capabilities, the partnership can achieve a deeper and more comprehensive understanding of complex problems.

5. Decision-Making and Trust: In the human-AI partnership, humans retain decision-making authority, while AI systems serve as valuable tools to support decision-making processes. Trust is crucial for an effective partnership, and it is built through transparency, explainability, and the ability to understand and interpret AI system outputs. Clear communication and interpretable AI systems foster trust and enable humans to confidently rely on AI-generated insights.

6. Ethical Considerations: The human-AI partnership necessitates ethical considerations. Humans must ensure that AI systems adhere to ethical guidelines, fairness, and accountability. They are responsible for monitoring AI systems, addressing biases, and ensuring the ethical use of AI technology. Ethical considerations play a crucial role in shaping the behavior and impact of AI systems within the partnership.

The human-AI partnership is not about replacing humans with AI but rather leveraging AI technology to enhance human capabilities and augment decision-making processes. By combining human intuition, creativity, and ethical judgment with AI's computational power and data analysis, the partnership can unlock new possibilities, improve efficiency, and drive innovation across various domains.

COLLABORATION AND COOPERATION WITH AI SYSTEMS

Collaboration and cooperation with AI systems involve working together with these systems to achieve common goals and leverage their capabilities effectively. Here are key considerations for successful collaboration:

1. Shared Goals: Establish shared goals and objectives between humans and AI systems. Clearly define the desired outcomes and align the efforts of both parties towards achieving those goals. This ensures a common understanding and promotes collaborative decision-making.
2. Communication and Interactions: Foster effective communication channels between humans and AI systems. Develop intuitive user interfaces, natural language interactions, and feedback mechanisms to facilitate seamless collaboration. Provide clear instructions and prompts to guide the AI system's behavior and enable users to provide input.
3. Mutual Understanding: Strive for mutual understanding between humans and AI systems. Humans should understand the capabilities and limitations of the AI system, while the AI system should comprehend the context, preferences, and goals of the humans it is collaborating with. This mutual understanding enhances cooperation and minimizes misunderstandings.
4. Task Allocation and Specialization: Allocate tasks and responsibilities based on the strengths and expertise of each party. Assign tasks that play to the strengths of the AI system, such as data analysis, pattern recognition, or automation, while reserving tasks requiring creativity,

critical thinking, and judgment for humans. Specialization enables efficient use of resources and maximizes overall performance.

5. Feedback and Iterative Improvement: Provide feedback loops to continuously improve the collaboration with AI systems. Humans can provide feedback on the AI system's outputs, performance, and behavior, allowing for iterative improvements. AI systems can also learn from human feedback to enhance their capabilities and adapt to user preferences over time.

6. Trust and Explainability: Foster trust in AI systems through transparency and explainability. Humans should have insight into the decision-making processes of the AI system, understand how it arrives at its outputs, and have the ability to interpret and validate those outputs. Explainable AI helps build trust and enables users to confidently rely on AI-generated insights.

7. Human Oversight and Responsibility: Maintain human oversight and accountability in the collaboration with AI systems. Humans should be responsible for ensuring ethical use, monitoring AI system behavior, and addressing any biases or unintended consequences that may arise. Human judgment and ethical considerations play a vital role in guiding the collaboration.

8. Continuous Learning and Adaptation: Embrace a culture of continuous learning and adaptation in the collaboration with AI systems. Both humans and AI systems should continuously learn from each other, adapt to changing circumstances, and incorporate new insights and knowledge into their respective roles. This enables continuous improvement and keeps the collaboration dynamic.

By fostering collaboration and cooperation with AI systems, organizations and individuals can harness the strengths of both humans and machines, leading to more effective problem-solving, improved decision-making, and enhanced overall performance. A balanced partnership ensures that AI systems are valuable tools that augment human capabilities, resulting in impactful and meaningful outcomes.

ENHANCING HUMAN CAPABILITIES WITH CHATGPT

ChatGPT can enhance human capabilities in various ways, providing valuable support and assistance. Here are some ways ChatGPT can enhance human capabilities:

1. Information Retrieval: ChatGPT can quickly retrieve relevant information from vast amounts of data. It can assist humans in conducting research, retrieving facts, and providing contextual information, saving time and effort.
2. Knowledge Expansion: ChatGPT has access to a wide range of knowledge and can provide insights, explanations, and answers to a diverse set of questions. It can help humans expand their knowledge base, learn new concepts, and stay informed on various topics.
3. Decision Support: ChatGPT can offer suggestions, recommendations, and alternative perspectives to aid humans in decision-making processes. It can analyze data, provide insights, and present potential options for consideration, assisting humans in making more informed choices.
4. Creative Inspiration: ChatGPT's generative capabilities can spark creativity and provide inspiration to human users. It can offer ideas, brainstorming prompts, and suggestions for various creative endeavors, such as writing, design, or problem-solving.
5. Language Assistance: ChatGPT can assist with language-related tasks, such as proofreading, grammar checks, and language refinement. It can provide language suggestions, help improve writing quality, and enhance overall communication skills.

6. Task Automation: ChatGPT can automate repetitive or mundane tasks, freeing up humans to focus on more complex and strategic activities. For example, it can handle routine customer inquiries, provide basic support, or automate data entry tasks.
7. Language Translation and Interpretation: ChatGPT's language capabilities enable it to assist with translation and interpretation tasks. It can facilitate communication between individuals who speak different languages, improving cross-cultural understanding and collaboration.
8. Personal Productivity: ChatGPT can act as a virtual assistant, helping humans manage their schedules, set reminders, and organize tasks. It can provide personalized recommendations, reminders, and productivity tips, enhancing individual efficiency and time management.
9. Supportive Dialogue and Emotional Well-being: ChatGPT can engage in supportive conversations, providing companionship and emotional support. It can listen to users, offer empathetic responses, and provide a non-judgmental space for individuals to express their thoughts and feelings.
10. Accessibility and Inclusivity: ChatGPT can assist individuals with disabilities or limitations, providing accessible interfaces and support for various tasks. It can help bridge communication gaps, offer assistance to those with visual or hearing impairments, and contribute to a more inclusive digital environment.

It's important to note that while ChatGPT can enhance human capabilities, it is meant to be a tool and should be used in collaboration with human judgment, critical thinking, and ethical considerations. The combined efforts of humans and ChatGPT can lead to more efficient and effective outcomes across a wide range of domains and tasks.

ETHICAL CONSIDERATIONS IN HUMAN-AI

Ethical considerations are crucial in the development and deployment of Human-AI systems to ensure their responsible and beneficial use. Here are key ethical considerations in the context of Human-AI collaboration:

1. Fairness and Bias: Pay attention to potential biases in AI systems and mitigate them to ensure fairness. Biases can arise from biased training data, unequal representation, or algorithmic design. Strive to provide fair treatment and equal opportunities to all individuals, avoiding discrimination and harmful biases.
2. Transparency and Explainability: Promote transparency and explainability in AI systems to build trust and accountability. Users should have a clear understanding of how AI systems make decisions, and the ability to interpret the rationale behind their outputs. Explainability helps identify and address potential biases or errors.
3. User Consent and Privacy: Obtain informed consent from users when collecting and processing their data. Safeguard user privacy and handle personal information responsibly. Be transparent about data collection, storage, and usage practices. Protect sensitive user information from unauthorized access or misuse.
4. Human Oversight and Responsibility: Ensure humans maintain oversight and ultimate decision-making authority in Human-AI collaborations. Humans should have the ability to question, challenge, and intervene when necessary. They are responsible for the actions and outcomes of AI systems and should exercise ethical judgment.
5. Accountability and Liability: Clearly define accountability and liability in Human-AI collaborations. Establish

guidelines for determining responsibility when issues or harm arise. Ensure that appropriate safeguards, monitoring mechanisms, and redress options are in place to address potential risks and mitigate harm.

6. Robustness and Safety: Develop AI systems with robustness and safety in mind. Take measures to prevent system vulnerabilities, ensure secure handling of user inputs and outputs, and address potential risks and failures. Regularly test and validate the system's behavior to minimize the likelihood of unintended consequences.

7. Socioeconomic Impact: Consider the broader societal impact of Human-AI collaborations. Strive for inclusivity, addressing potential disparities and inequalities arising from the use of AI systems. Assess and mitigate any negative socioeconomic consequences, and work towards solutions that promote positive societal outcomes.

8. Ethical Use and Misuse: Promote the ethical use of AI systems and guard against potential misuse. Ensure that AI systems are used in ways that respect human rights, do not harm individuals or communities, and conform to legal and ethical standards. Proactively prevent the development and deployment of AI systems for malicious purposes.

9. Continuous Monitoring and Improvement: Regularly monitor and evaluate Human-AI systems to identify and address ethical concerns. Engage in ongoing dialogue with users, stakeholders, and the broader public to gather feedback, consider diverse perspectives, and make improvements that align with societal values.

10. Collaboration and Multidisciplinary Perspectives: Foster collaboration across disciplines, involving experts in ethics, law, social sciences, and other relevant fields. Engage in multidisciplinary discussions to address ethical challenges holistically, considering diverse perspectives and ethical frameworks.

By prioritizing ethical considerations in Human-AI collaborations, we can ensure that AI systems are developed, deployed, and used in ways that benefit society, uphold fundamental values, and respect the rights and dignity of individuals. Responsible and ethical practices are essential for building trust, minimizing harm, and harnessing the full potential of AI technology for the betterment of humanity.

RECAP OF KEY POINTS

Certainly! Here's a recap of the key points discussed:

1. Human-AI Partnership: The human-AI partnership involves collaboration and cooperation between humans and AI systems to leverage their respective strengths and capabilities for more effective outcomes.
2. Enhancing Human Capabilities with ChatGPT: ChatGPT can enhance human capabilities through information retrieval, knowledge expansion, decision support, creative inspiration, language assistance, task automation, language translation, and interpretation, personal productivity, and supportive dialogue.
3. Ethical Considerations: Ethical considerations in Human-AI collaboration include fairness and bias mitigation, transparency and explainability, user consent and privacy, human oversight and responsibility, accountability and liability, robustness and safety, socioeconomic impact, ethical use and misuse prevention, continuous monitoring and improvement, and collaboration with multidisciplinary perspectives.
4. User Feedback and Improving ChatGPT: Collecting user feedback helps in identifying issues, biases, and areas for improvement. OpenAI encourages users to provide feedback, which is analyzed and incorporated to refine ChatGPT over time.
5. Challenges in User Feedback: Challenges in user feedback include limited quantity, biased subset of users, vague or incomplete feedback, difficulty in extracting actionable insights, conflicting feedback, incorporating feedback in a timely manner, balancing user preferences and ethical considerations, and communicating updates to users.

6. Human-AI Collaboration: Successful human-AI collaboration involves shared goals, effective communication and interactions, mutual understanding, task allocation and specialization, feedback and iterative improvement, trust and explainability, human oversight and responsibility, and continuous learning and adaptation.

7. Responsible Use of ChatGPT: Responsible use of ChatGPT entails addressing biases and fairness, ensuring transparency and accountability, protecting user privacy, promoting human judgment and decision-making, and actively monitoring and managing potential risks.

8. Privacy and Security Concerns: Considerations around privacy and security involve safeguarding user data, implementing secure storage and transmission, and following best practices to protect user information from unauthorized access or misuse.

9. Mitigating Potential Risks: Mitigating potential risks involves proactive measures such as robust testing, vulnerability identification and remediation, ongoing monitoring, and addressing safety concerns to ensure the reliable and secure operation of AI systems.

10. Future of ChatGPT: The future of ChatGPT involves ongoing research, development, and improvement efforts by OpenAI, including advancements in training techniques, model architectures, and addressing limitations to enhance the capabilities and impact of ChatGPT.

These points provide a comprehensive overview of the discussed topics.

REFLECTIONS ON THE FUTURE OF CHATGPT

The future of ChatGPT holds immense potential for further advancements and impact. Reflecting on its future, here are some key considerations:

1. Enhanced Language Understanding: Future iterations of ChatGPT are likely to exhibit improved language understanding capabilities. This includes better comprehension of context, nuances, and user intent, leading to more accurate and contextually appropriate responses.

2. Domain-Specific Expertise: ChatGPT could be tailored and fine-tuned for specific domains, allowing it to provide more specialized and accurate information in areas such as medicine, law, finance, or technology. This would enable users to access domain-specific expertise quickly and efficiently.

3. Customization and Personalization: The ability to personalize ChatGPT's behavior and responses could become more prevalent. Users may have greater control over the chatbot's tone, style, and recommendations, making the interaction feel more tailored to individual preferences.

4. Multimodal Capabilities: Future versions of ChatGPT may extend beyond text-based interactions and incorporate multimodal capabilities, allowing it to understand and generate responses incorporating visual or auditory elements. This could enable more immersive and interactive experiences.

5. Contextual Adaptation: ChatGPT could evolve to better adapt to changing conversation dynamics and user needs. It may employ techniques such as tracking dialogue history,

remembering user preferences, and adjusting responses based on the evolving context to provide more coherent and personalized interactions.

6. Ethical and Bias Mitigation: OpenAI's commitment to addressing biases and ensuring ethical use is likely to continue. Future iterations of ChatGPT may incorporate enhanced mechanisms for bias detection and mitigation, as well as features that enable users to actively influence and shape the ethical behavior of the chatbot.

7. Collaborative Problem Solving: ChatGPT could facilitate collaborative problem-solving by enabling multiple users to interact with it simultaneously. This could lead to collaborative brainstorming, group decision-making, and knowledge sharing, amplifying the collective intelligence of human-AI collaborations.

8. Enhanced User Feedback Loop: OpenAI's dedication to user feedback and iterative improvement will likely continue to drive enhancements in ChatGPT. Further improvements in collecting, analyzing, and incorporating user feedback will help shape future iterations and make the chatbot more responsive to user needs.

9. Responsible Development and Deployment: As the adoption of AI systems increases, responsible development and deployment practices will be paramount. OpenAI will continue to prioritize addressing ethical concerns, ensuring transparency, and adhering to best practices to mitigate potential risks and promote responsible use of ChatGPT.

10. Integration into Everyday Life: With advancements and improvements, ChatGPT has the potential to become an integral part of people's daily lives. From personal assistants to educational tools, customer support, and creative collaboration, ChatGPT could seamlessly integrate into various industries and domains.

The future of ChatGPT holds exciting possibilities, with continuous advancements driven by user feedback, research breakthroughs, and ethical considerations. As it evolves, ChatGPT has the potential to transform the way we interact with AI systems and unlock new opportunities for collaboration, knowledge sharing, and problem-solving.

FINAL THOUGHTS AND RECOMMENDATIONS

In conclusion, ChatGPT represents a significant milestone in the development of conversational AI systems. Its ability to engage in human-like conversations and provide valuable support showcases the potential of AI technology in enhancing human capabilities. However, it is essential to approach the use of ChatGPT and similar AI systems with careful consideration and responsible practices. Here are some final thoughts and recommendations:

1. Embrace Collaboration: Emphasize the collaboration between humans and AI systems rather than viewing them as replacements for one another. The human-AI partnership can lead to more effective outcomes by leveraging the strengths of both entities.
2. User-Centric Design: Prioritize user needs, expectations, and feedback throughout the development and deployment of AI systems. Regularly seek user feedback, actively listen to their concerns, and iterate on the system to continuously improve its performance and user experience.
3. Address Bias and Ethical Concerns: Proactively address biases and ethical considerations to ensure fairness, inclusivity, and unbiased behavior of AI systems. Strive for transparency, explainability, and accountability to build trust and mitigate potential risks.
4. Responsible Use: Use AI systems responsibly and consider their potential impact on individuals, communities, and society as a whole. Ensure compliance with privacy regulations, protect user data, and guard against the misuse of AI technology.

5. Continuous Improvement: Embrace a culture of continuous learning, innovation, and improvement. Invest in research and development efforts to advance AI technology, enhance its capabilities, and address limitations or challenges.
6. Interdisciplinary Collaboration: Encourage collaboration across diverse disciplines such as computer science, ethics, social sciences, and policy-making. This collaboration ensures a holistic understanding of the implications and societal impact of AI systems.
7. Education and Awareness: Promote education and awareness about AI technology, its capabilities, and its limitations among the general public, policymakers, and stakeholders. Foster an informed dialogue that encourages responsible adoption and usage of AI systems.
8. Emphasize Human Values: Ensure that the development and deployment of AI systems align with human values, respect human rights, and prioritize human well-being. Human judgment, ethics, and decision-making should always be at the forefront of AI applications.

As AI technology continues to evolve, it is important to navigate the possibilities and challenges it presents with a commitment to ethics, inclusivity, and responsible practices. By embracing the potential of AI systems while upholding human values, we can harness the benefits of this technology and create a future that is beneficial for all.